# AI/ML Demystified

**A Comprehensive Guide to the Risks, Challenges and Opportunities**

Aruna Joshi, Ph.D., FRM

.

Published in USA


Cover Design: GetCovers.com

Editors: Sunanda Chatterjee, Arun Majumdar and Ajit Mayya

*This book is dedicated to my husband, Arun Majumdar whose encouragement and persistence made this book a reality and my parents Avinash and Mandakini Joshi who have been my constant support through life's ups and downs.*

# Table of Contents

# Chapter 1: What's the Big Deal about AI/ML

*"The potential benefits of artificial intelligence are huge, so are the dangers." – Dave Waters*

You may have noticed that if you search for a product, say, "Instant Pot," or "Fitbit" in your web browser, or are searching for flights to say, "Tahiti", you get flooded with advertisements related to these searches. Interestingly, they seem to follow you even when you visit *other* websites. Or when you search for "tennis" on YouTube, , tennis shows up more often than anything else.

Behind the scenes there is an algorithm that is predicting your behavior or interests. This algorithm usually falls under the category of **Artificial Intelligence** (AI) or **Machine Learning** (ML).

**Artificial intelligence** (AI) is the ability of a computer or a machine controlled by a computer to do tasks that are usually done by humans because they require human intelligence and discernment.

**Machine learning** (ML) is a type of artificial intelligence (AI) that allows software applications to become more accurate at predicting outcomes. Machine learning algorithms use historical data as input to predict future outcomes. It is a branch of AI based on the idea that systems can learn from data, identify patterns and make decisions with minimal human intervention.

Some examples of AI include Apple Siri, Google Assistant and Amazon Alexa. Examples of ML include stock prediction, recommendations like we saw above and estimating fraud probability of a financial transaction.

I joined the financial services industry more than a decade ago as a **quant**[1] in the Risk Management department and am extremely familiar with mathematical and statistical techniques called "models" that fall under AI and ML. Although the financial services industry is heavily regulated and adoption of such models is at a slower pace than other industries like hi-tech, such models are now finding their way in healthcare, agriculture, and in hospitality.

A few changes have led to dramatic progress in AI/ML: (a) marked increase in computer memory and computational power; (b) decreasing cost of computing and (c) availability of terabytes of data that can be used to develop models. Because of changes, these AL/ML techniques are becoming ubiquitous and are showing up in areas previously unheard of, such as detecting cancer from images, or opening a bank account without ever visiting a bank in person, or riding in a driverless car!

Even if you're not in the hi-tech or financial services industry, but are curious as to how these AI-ML models are built, this book is for you.

---

[1] An expert at analyzing and managing quantitative data

Unfortunately, these models may also pose risks and their use can result in unintentional consequences and/or harm.

Let us consider a couple of case studies where AI/ML models caused what could be considered as some harm to society. The first example is related to privacy and the second example is related to the risk of automation with no human in the loop to make decisions.

---

In 2012, a man walked into a Target outside Minneapolis and demanded to see the manager. He was clutching coupons that had been sent to his daughter, and he was angry, according to an employee who participated in the conversation.

"My daughter got this in the mail!" he said. "She's still in high school, and you're sending her coupons for baby clothes and cribs? Are you trying to encourage her to get pregnant?"

The manager didn't have any idea what the man was talking about. He looked at the mailer. Sure enough, it was addressed to the man's daughter and contained advertisements for maternity clothing, nursery furniture and pictures of smiling infants. The manager apologized and then called a few days later to apologize again.

On the phone, though, the father was somewhat abashed. "I had a talk with my daughter," he said. "It turns out there's been some activities in my house I haven't been completely aware of. She's due in August. I owe you an apology."

What happened here is that every time you go shopping, you share intimate details about your consumption patterns with retailers. And many of those retailers are studying those details to figure out what you like, what you need, and which coupons are most likely to make you happy. Target, for example, has figured out how to data-mine its way into your womb, to figure out whether you have a baby on the way long before you need to start buying diapers.

Source:
https://www.nytimes.com/2012/02/19/magazine/shopping-habits.html?_r=1&hp=&pagewanted=all

Amazon.com Inc's AMZN.O machine-learning specialists uncovered a big problem: their new recruiting engine did not like women.

The team had been building computer algorithms since 2014 to review job applicants' resumes with the aim of mechanizing the search for top talent, five people familiar with the effort told Reuters.

Automation has been key to Amazon's e-commerce dominance, be it inside warehouses or driving pricing decisions. The company's experimental hiring tool used artificial intelligence to give job candidates scores ranging from one to five stars - much like shoppers rate products on Amazon, some of the people said.

"Everyone wanted this holy grail," one of the employees familiar with the effort said. "They literally wanted it to be an engine where I'm going to give you 100 resumes, it will spit out the top five, and we'll hire those."

But by 2015, the company realized its new system was not rating candidates for software developer jobs and other technical posts in a gender-neutral manner. That is because Amazon's computer models were trained to vet applicants by observing patterns in resumes submitted to the company over a 10-year period. Most came from men, a reflection of male dominance across the tech industry.

In effect, Amazon's algorithm taught itself that male candidates were preferable. It penalized resumes that included the word "women's," as in "women's chess club captain." And it downgraded graduates of two all-women's colleges, according to people familiar with the matter. They did not specify the names of the schools.

Amazon edited the programs to make them neutral to these particular terms. But that was no guarantee that the machines would not devise other ways of sorting candidates that could prove discriminatory, the people said.

The Seattle company ultimately disbanded the team by the start of last year because executives lost hope for the project, according to the people, who spoke on condition of anonymity. Amazon's recruiters looked at the recommendations generated by the tool when searching for new hires, but never relied solely on those rankings, they said.

Source: https://www.reuters.com/article/us-amazon-com-jobs-automation-insight-idUSKCN1MK08G

The above case studies underscore the risks of AI and ML applications. As you browse the news articles, you will notice that AI and ML is cropping up with a higher frequency whether it is related to simple tasks like telephonic customer service or self-driving cars and most recently, ChatGPT.

In this book, I first describe what artificial intelligence, machine learning and data science mean in layman terms. I then describe in simple terms how a data scientist builds such models. Those chapters also have some optional sections that go into detail on some methodologies if you choose to dig deeper.

I will then delve into how practitioners assess risks posed by these models and how to mitigate these risks. I will also use several relatable examples.

The final chapter is devoted to the latest AI craze called ChatGPT and similar large-language models.

# Chapter 2: AI, MI, Deep Learning

*"Machine Intelligence is the last invention that humanity will have to need to make."--- Nick Bostrom*

### Artificial Intelligence (AI)

Artificial intelligence (AI) refers to the simulation of human intelligence in machines that are programmed to think like humans and mimic their actions.

Figure **1** below depicts the history of AI.

### Figure 1: History of AI

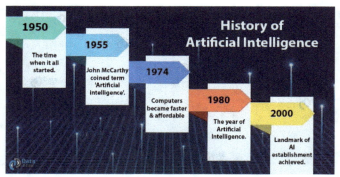

Source: https://data-flair.training/blogs/history-of-artificial-intelligence/

**1950 – The time when it all started (: Baby Is Born)**

In 1950, the English Mathematician Alan Turing published a paper entitled "Computing Machinery and Intelligence" which opened the doors to a new and exciting field.

**1956 – When it was defined (The Baby is Named)**

The term "Artificial Intelligence" was coined in 1956 by Stanford professor John McCarthy at the Dartmouth Summer Research Project on Artificial Intelligence. This summer workshop is widely considered to be the founding event of artificial intelligence as a field organized by John McCarthy with participants: Marvin Minsky, Nathaniel Rochester, and Claude Shannon (who proposed the workshop), and others.

It is little wonder that John McCarthy, the prominent computer and cognitive scientist is considered as the Father of AI. McCarthy would define AI as "the science and engineering of making intelligent machines".

**1974 – Computers flourished! (The Baby Grows)**

The wave of computers started gradually. With time, they became faster, more affordable, and able to store more information. Machine learning algorithms improved and programmers became better at knowing which algorithm to apply to the problem they were trying to solve. However, computers could not store enough information or process it fast enough and funding and research slowed down.

**1980 – The year of AI (Baby's Coming of Age)**

In 1980, AI research got re-vitalized with an expansion of not only funding by Japanese government as part of their Fifth Generation Computer Project (FGCP)[2] but also algorithmic tools such as deep learning technique — (to be explained later in the book) — Computer programmers were able to make the computers mimic human behavior such as distinguishing between cats and birds and performing complex activities such as in a manufacturing facility through the use of data.

**2000's –Landmark achieved (Baby becomes an Adult)**

It was not until the 2000s that the landmark goals of using artificial intelligence for practical purposes was achieved. Earlier, AI thrived in predominantly research environments.

Now, AI applications can be found everywhere, for example,

- Chatbots that analyze customer requests and answer them.
- Recommendations for content for viewers/consumers based on other content they have consumed/purchased.
- Self-driving cars and robots used for delivery.

**Machine Learning (ML)**

Machine learning (ML) is a subset of AI where you use historical data as input into an algorithm to *predict* new output values.

---

[2] https://www.nytimes.com/1984/11/12/business/japan-gain-reported-in-computers.html

The term "Machine Learning" was coined by a computer science professor, Oren Etzioni, and computer scientists Michele Banko and Michael Cafarella.

Machine learning algorithms are used in a wide variety of applications, such as in medicine, email filtering, speech recognition, and computer vision. In simple terms, ML algorithms are used where it is difficult or unfeasible to develop conventional algorithms to perform the needed tasks.

### Deep Learning

Deep Learning is a subset of ML, which uses artificial neural networks or ANNs (described more in detail in Chapter 5) that attempt to simulate the behavior of the human brain allowing it to "learn" from large amounts of data.

### Figure 2: AI, ML and Deep Learning

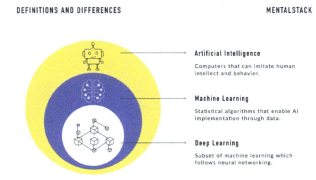

DEFINITIONS AND DIFFERENCES    MENTALSTACK

**Artificial Intelligence**
Computers that can imitate human intellect and behavior.

**Machine Learning**
Statistical algorithms that enable AI implementation through data.

**Deep Learning**
Subset of machine learning which follows neural networking.

Source: https://mentalstack.com/blog/ai-vs-ml-vs-dl

## Key Takeaways

- Artificial Intelligence (AI) refers to the simulation of human intelligence in machines that are programmed to think like humans and mimic their actions
- Although the term Artificial Intelligence was coined in 1956 by Stanford Professor John McCarthy, it took almost 50 years for computational power to increase significantly and storage to become cheap before AI could be used for practical purposes
- Machine Learning (ML) is a subset of Artificial Intelligence where you use historical data as input into an algorithm to predict new output values
- Deep Learning is a subset of ML which uses artificial neural networks that attempt to simulate the behavior of the human brans allowing it to "learn" from large amount of

# Chapter 3: Simple ML models

*"I'm no model lady. A model's just an imitation of the real thing."– Mae West*

What is a model?

A **model** is defined as a process that consists of three components:

- an **information input component**, which delivers assumptions and data to the process;
- a **processing component**, which transforms inputs into estimates using statistical, mathematical, etc. theories;
- a **reporting component**, which translates the estimates into useful information such as forecasts or estimates

**Figure 3: Model Definition**

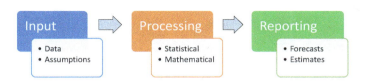

If the quantitative process meets all the components, the process is deemed to be a **model**.

## Linear Regression

The simplest machine models that most high school students have probably come across are simple linear models. In these models, you try to find a relationship between an independent variable $x$, say height of a person, to a dependent variable $y$, say weight of that person. The equation that represents such relationship is

$$y = mx + b$$

Where $m$ is called the slope and $b$ is called the intercept (value of $y$ when $x = 0$). If $x$ increases by 1 unit, $y$ increases by $m$ units. In Figure **4**, for the 5 datapoints for height and weight, the best line shows m = 4.8635 and b = -169.32.

**Figure 4: Schematic of Linear Regression**

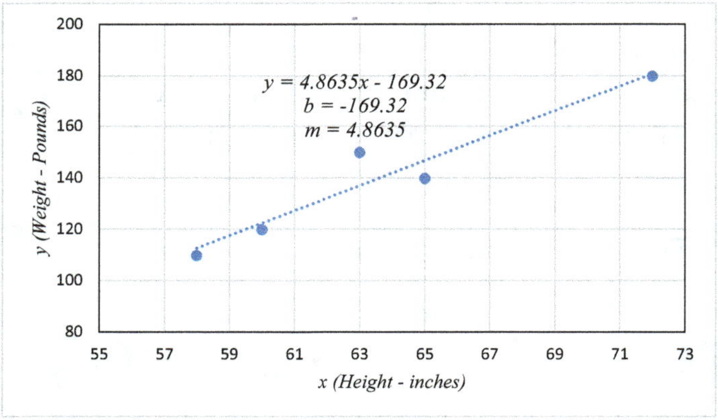

*Optional Reading for a Deeper Dive*

Consider a dataset of 10,000 historical measurements of height and weight for men and women (5,000 for men and 5,000 for women) available for download from https://www.kaggle.com/datasets/mustafaali96/weight-height?resource=download

**Table 1: Height (inches) vs. Weight (pounds) for Males and Females**

| Data Point | Gender | Height | Weight |
|:---:|:---|:---:|:---:|
| i | | x | y |
| 1 | Male | 73.84702 | 241.8936 |
| 2 | Male | 68.7819 | 162.3105 |
| 3 | Male | 74.11011 | 212.7409 |
| 4 | Male | 71.73098 | 220.0425 |
| 5 | Male | 69.8818 | 206.3498 |
| 6 | Male | 67.25302 | 152.2122 |
| 7 | Male | 68.78508 | 183.9279 |
| 8 | Male | 68.34852 | 167.9711 |
| 9 | Male | 67.01895 | 175.9294 |
| 10 | Male | 63.45649 | 156.3997 |
| 11 | Male | 71.19538 | 186.6049 |
| 12 | Male | 71.64081 | 213.7412 |
| 13 | Male | 64.76633 | 167.1275 |

*After downloading the datasets, you can draw a chart showing the distribution of height versus weights for males and females (Figure 5)*

**Figure 5: Height vs. Weight for Male and Female**

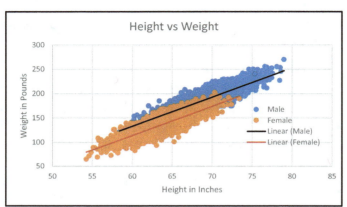

Looking at the blue and orange points for males and females respectively, we can generate trendlines for both assuming a linear relationship and would be able to say that a woman who is 5 ft 5 inches tall (65 inches) probably weighs somewhere close to 150 lb (by looking at the red trendline) and a man with the same height probably weighs around 160 lb (by looking at the black trendline). We created the trendlines assuming a linear relationship between height and weight (meaning that when we increase the height by one unit, the weight increases by an amount equal to slope of the line, m as mentioned before). The slope and intercept (m and b respectively) are determined by an optimization technique where we minimize the difference or error between actual and predicted dependent variable (also based on certain criteria using the equation

predicted weight = m*actual height + b

for all data points. The most common type of error to be minimized (predicted weight – actual weight) is defined as the average of the sum of error-squared defined as

$Mean\ squared\ error$

$$= \frac{1}{n} \sum_{i=1}^{n} (y, predicted_i - y, actual_i)^2$$

*Where n is the total number of data points (5000 each for male and female), y,predicted is the ith value of the predicted variable, y,actual$_i$ is the ith value of the actual predicted variable.*

*Several techniques exist to minimize the mean squared error including an analytical method. If you have learned calculus, you may recall that when you want to minimize a function with two variables, you set the partial derivative of the function with respect to each variable equal to 0. This will give you two equations and you can solve for m and b.*

*The analytical result for m and b using the above analytical method is*

$$m = \frac{S_{xy}}{S_{xx}}$$

*b = (mean of y) – (mean of x)*m*

*where*

$$S_{xx} = \sum x^2 - \frac{(\sum x)^2}{n}$$

$$S_{yy} = \sum y^2 - \frac{(\sum y)^2}{n}$$

$$Sxy = \sum xy - \frac{(\sum x)(\sum y)}{n}$$

*mean of x = (sum of x)/n*

*mean of y = (sum of y)/n*

*In reality you may have hundreds of datapoints making the analytical method cumbersome. In such cases, you can either use a Python library, an Excel formula.*

*This is the simplest type of a machine learning model. These types of models have been in use for decades since they do not require much computing power and are referred to as linear regression models.*

*Businesses often use linear regression to understand the relationship between, for example, advertising spending and revenue. For example, they might fit a simple linear regression model using advertising spending as the predictor variable and revenue as the response variable. The regression model would take the following form:*

*revenue = m\* ad spending + b*

*The intercept b would represent total expected revenue when ad spending is zero.*

*Another application is when medical researchers use linear regression to understand the relationship between drug dosage and blood pressure of patients. For example, researchers might administer various dosages of a certain drug to patients and observe how their blood pressure responds. They might fit a simple linear regression model using dosage as the predictor variable and blood pressure as the response variable. The regression model would take the following form:*

*blood pressure = m\*dosage + b*

*The intercept b would represent the expected blood pressure when dosage is zero.*

*A closely related type of model is a multiple linear regression model where instead of one independent variable, you use multiple independent variables to predict the dependent variable. For example, to try to predict blood pressure (the dependent variable) you may use independent variables such as height, weight, age, gender, and hours of exercise per week in addition to the dosage as your independent variables. Such equations are denoted as*

$$y = m_1 x_1 + m_2 x_2 + \cdots m_i x_i + \cdots + m_n x_n b$$

*Where $m_1$, $m_2$, $m_i$ etc. are slopes for the independent variables, $x_1$, $x_2$, $x_i$ etc., n is the total number of independent variables and b is the intercept. The cost function, error to be minimized in the equation above remains the same but we use $x_1$, $x_2$, $x_i ... x_n$ to determine the dependent variable y. We covered earlier in the section on how the error is minimized.*

*So we found the coefficients for which the error is minimized but how do we determine how good the model is? Well, for linear regression models, typically a measure or metric called R-squared ($R^2$) is evaluated. .*

*$R^2$ explains to what extent the variation of independent variables explains the variation of the dependent variable. So, if the $R^2$ of a model is 0.50, then approximately half of the*

*observed variation can be explained by the model's inputs. So the closer $R^2$ is to 1, the better the model.*

*The formula for calculating $R^2$ is*

$$R^2 = 1 - \left(\frac{SSR}{SST}\right) = 1 - \frac{\sum_{i=1}^{n}(y_i - \hat{y}_i)^2}{\sum_{i=1}^{n}(y_i - \bar{y})^2}$$

*Where SSR = sum squared residuals and SST is the total sum of squares (i.e., the sum of squared deviations from the mean).*

*n is the total number of datapoints, $y_i$ is the ith datapoint, $\hat{y}_i$ is the predicted value of y at ith datapoint and $\bar{y}$ is the average of y.*

### Classification Problem

Another type of a machine learning model widely used is a classification model. Such a model reads or takes in some input data and generates an output that classifies the input into some categories.

For example, a classification model might read an email and classify it as either spam or not (binary classification since the output is binary) based on certain attributes such as sender's country, number of recipients, etc.

Or from a collection of images, a model may separate fruits into groups e.g., apples, mangoes and limes, based on different attributes, such as color, taste, shape etc. Since the final solution is not binary, it is also called a multi-classifier.

Finally, in the financial services industry, a model might look at several attributes related to a payment transaction of a credit card such as payment amount, history of the card holder with the merchant, how many transactions have been made with the card in the last 24 hours etc. to determine the probability that the transaction may be fraudulent.

**The key in classification problems is that the final answer of the dataset is known** (in the data that was used to train the model or what you are trying to predict).

For example, in the spam/no spam case, all data points have a label associated with them, e.g., "spam" or "not spam." In the multi-classifier case, all data points have a label associated with them such as "apple", "mango" or "lime" and finally in the fraud model, whether the transaction is fraudulent or not.

Let us get familiar with a couple of terms in relation to machine learning models: 1) **feature** – this is the input into the model e.g., source or email or content for the spam filter or color, shape/color of the fruit for the fruit classifier, transaction amount, history with the merchant etc. for the fraud model; and 2) **label** – this is the output of the model e.g., spam or not spam, apple, mango or lime, and fraud or not fraud for the examples described above.

**Figure 6: Spam Email Binary Classifier**

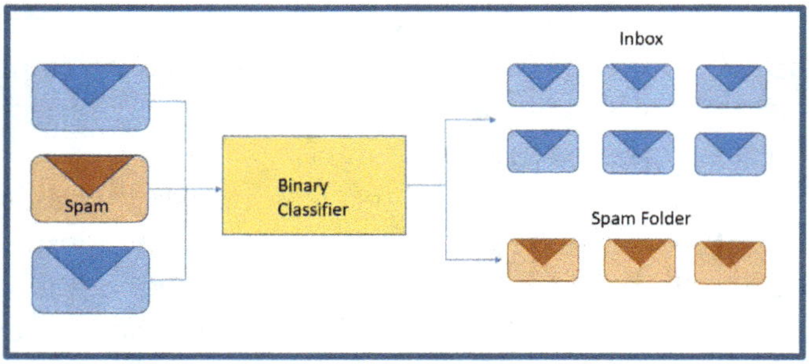

### Figure 7: Multi-class classifier

## *Optional Reading for a Deeper Dive*

*The simplest way to solve a classification problem that has been widely used in the financial services industry is **logistic regression**. This is closely associated with linear regression, except the solution represents a probability (e.g., fraud) and hence is always bounded between 0 and 1.*

*The logistic regression equation can be written as*

$$ln\frac{p}{1-p} = m_0 + m_1x_1 + m_2x_2 + \cdots m_ix_i + \cdots$$
$$+ m_nx_nb$$

*Where ln is the natural logarithm, p is the probability of an event occurring, $x_i$ are the input features and $m_i$ are the coefficients.*

*So how do we apply the result of the logistic regression to a binary problem?*

*The problem we are trying to solve is that of an event occurring or not occurring. However, our solution is a probability, or a number between 0 and 1. So how do we translate the probability into determining whether we predict an even to occur or not?*

*We apply a cut-off, c where we assume if the calculated probability is higher than c, the model will classify that data point to the event occurring. Say, the cutoff is 0.5 or 50% probability. If for a particular data point (combination of features), the calculated probability from the model is 0.65, we assume that the event has occurred.*

*Based on the cutoff, we come up with a matrix called a* **confusion matrix** *as depicted below. A confusion matrix is a table that is used to define the performance of a classification algorithm. A confusion matrix visualizes and summarizes the performance of a classification problem.*

**Figure 8: Confusion Matrix**

|  | Actually Positive (1) | Actually Negative (0) |
|---|---|---|
| Predicted Positive (1) | True Positives (TPs) | False Positives (FPs) |
| Predicted Negative (0) | False Negatives (FNs) | True Negatives (TNs) |

*From the confusion matrix, two metrics are usually calculated:*

$$Sensitivity = \frac{TP}{TP+FN}$$

$$And\ Specificity = \frac{TN}{FP+TN}.$$

*In general, you would want both high sensitivity and high specificity.*

**Confusion matrix is often used in choosing a test for disease diagnosis such as COVID testing or tuberculosis testing. However, for low prevalence diseases such as tuberculosis in the US, the false negative rate will be low and the false positive rate will be high. For high prevalence diseases such as tuberculosis in India, the false negative rate will be high and the false positive rate will be lower.**

*As mentioned earlier, for linear regression, typically we look at $R^2$ to determine how good the fit of the model is. For logistic regression, there are several metrics, the most common being*

*Area Under the Receiver Operating Characteristic curve (AUROC) or ROC.*

*The ROC curve is a simple plot that shows the tradeoff between the true positive rate and the false positive rate of a classifier for various choices of the probability thresholds or cutoffs as shown below.*

*A random classifier (a model with predictive power similar to a random classifier) is a 45 degree line (red line shown below). A classifier that is better than the random will be a convex curve upwards as the orange, green or blue lines. The quicker the curve lifts, the better is the mode. The AUROC is the area under the curve. A random classifier has an AUC of 0.5 and a perfect classifier has an AUC of 1.0.*

### *Figure 9: Simple ROC Curve*

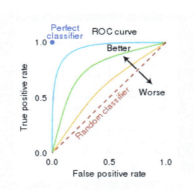

*There are several packages in Python that can generate such curves.*

### Clustering Problems

Clustering analysis is a technique used in machine learning that attempts to find clusters of observations within a dataset such that the observations within each cluster are quite similar to each other, while observations in different clusters are quite different from each other.

The most common applications of clustering are in retail marketing and streaming services.

For example, a retail company may collect the following information on households:

- Household income
- Household size
- Head of household occupation
- Distance from nearest urban area

They can then feed these variables into a clustering algorithm to send personalized advertisements or sales letters to each household based on how likely they are to respond to specific types of advertisements. Examples of clusters they may use are:

Cluster 1: Small family, high spenders

Cluster 2: Larger family, high spenders

Cluster 3: Small family, low spenders

Cluster 4: Large family, low spenders

Another example is streaming services often use clustering analysis to identify viewers who have similar behavior.

For example, a streaming service may collect the following data about individuals:

- Minutes watched per day
- Total viewing sessions per week
- Number of unique shows viewed per month

Using these metrics, a streaming service can perform cluster analysis to identify high usage and low usage users so that they can know who they should spend most of their advertising dollars on.

*Optional: Most Common Clustering Algorithm*

*One of the most popular machine learning algorithms used for clustering is called **K-Means**.*

***K-Means Clustering*** *groups the unlabeled dataset (example of retail and streaming services data that do not have any labels as opposed to the example of spam vs. non-spam email discussed earlier) into different clusters. Here K defines the number of pre-defined clusters that need to be created in the process, e.g., if K=2, there will be two clusters, and for K=3, there will be three clusters, and so on.*

*It is an iterative algorithm that divides the unlabeled dataset into k different clusters in such a way that each dataset belongs to only one group that has similar properties. The main aim of this algorithm is to minimize the sum of distances between the data point and their corresponding clusters.*

***Figure 10*** *below for a simple illustration of household size and household income represented by x and y axes respectively. The green dots show the distribution of data points.*

### Figure 10: K-means Example

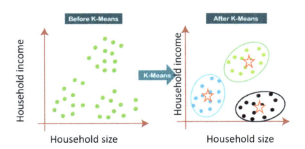

*K-Means algorithm follows the steps explained below:*
*Step-1: Select the number K to decide the number of clusters (for example above K = 3).*

*Step-2: Select random K points represented by red stars placed* ☆ *at approximately the center of the cluster known as centroid*
*Step-3: Assign each data point to their closest centroid which will form the predefined K clusters.*
*Step-4: Calculate the sum square distance of each point of the cluster from the centroid. Then place a new centroid in each cluster.*
*Step-5: Repeat the steps, which means reassign each datapoint to the new closest centroid of each cluster.*
*Step-6: If any reassignment occurs, then go to step-4 else go to FINISH.*
*Step-7: The model is ready.*

**The above technique can also be used in separating normal and abnormal white blood cells on the basis of size and granularity from images of blood cells.**

### Natural Language Processing

Natural language processing (NLP) focuses on enabling computers to understand, interpret, and generate human language. With the exponential growth of digital data and the increasing use of natural language interfaces, NLP has become a crucial technology for many businesses.

NLP technologies can be used for a wide range of applications, including sentiment analysis[3], chatbots, speech recognition, and translation, to mention a few. By leveraging NLP, businesses can automate tasks, improve customer service, and

---

[3] Sentiment analysis is the process of analyzing digital text to determine if the emotional tone of the message is positive, negative, or neutral

gain valuable insights from customer feedback and social media posts.

One of the key challenges in implementing NLP is dealing with the complexity and ambiguity of human language. NLP algorithms need to be trained on large amounts of data in order to recognize patterns and learn the nuances of language. They also need to be continually refined and updated to keep up with changes in language, slang use and context.

The technology works by breaking down language inputs, such as sentences or paragraphs, into smaller components and analyzing their meanings and relationships to generate insights or responses.

Since the process of understanding and manipulating language is extremely complex, it is common to use different techniques to handle different challenges before binding everything together.

**NLP technologies use a combination of techniques, including statistical modeling, machine learning, and deep learning, to recognize patterns and learn from large amounts of data in order to accurately interpret and generate language.**

*Optional: Frequently used NLP algorithms*
Below are some of the most frequently used algorithms in NLP:

## Bag of Words (BOW)

*The bag-of-words model is commonly used in methods of document classification where the frequency of occurrence of each word is used as a feature for training a classifier.*

*It involves two things:*

1. *A vocabulary of known words: This step revolves around constructing a document corpus which consists of all the unique words in the whole of the text present in the data provided. It is a dictionary of sorts where each index will correspond to one word and each word is a different dimension.*

   *Let us look at an example for a pizzeria with 4 reviews:*
   *Review #1 : This pizza is very tasty and affordable.*
   *Review #2: This pizza is not tasty but is affordable.*
   *Review #3 : This pizza is delicious and cheap.*
   *Review #4: Pizza is tasty and pizza tastes good.*

   *Now if we count the number of unique words in all the four reviews we end up with a total of 13 unique words. Below are the 13 unique words that form a vector of 13 dimensions:*
   *['This', 'pizza', 'is', 'very', 'tasty', 'and', 'affordable', 'not', 'but', 'delicious', 'cheap', 'tastes', 'good']*

2. *A measure of the presence of known words: We look at all reviews and count the number of times a word occurs in each review in the below table. Here the word 'is' appears twice in review 2 and the word pizza appears twice in review 4. All other words either appear once or not at all indicated by 0.*

**Table 2: Word frequency**

| Index/Dimension | Words | Freq #1 | Freq #2 | Freq #3 | Freq #4 |
|---|---|---|---|---|---|
| 1 | This | 1 | 1 | 1 | 0 |
| 2 | pizza | 1 | 1 | 1 | 2 |
| 3 | is | 1 | 2 | 1 | 1 |
| 4 | very | 1 | 0 | 0 | 0 |
| 5 | tasty | 1 | 1 | 0 | 1 |
| 6 | and | 1 | 0 | 1 | 1 |
| 7 | affordable | 1 | 1 | 0 | 0 |
| 8 | not | 0 | 1 | 0 | 0 |
| 9 | but | 0 | 1 | 0 | 0 |
| 10 | delicious | 0 | 0 | 1 | 0 |
| 11 | cheap | 0 | 0 | 1 | 0 |
| 12 | tastes | 0 | 0 | 0 | 1 |
| 13 | good | 0 | 0 | 0 | 1 |

After converting the reviews into such vectors we can compare different sentences by calculating the Euclidean distance between them to check if two reviews are similar or not. Euclidean distance between reviews is calculated by summing up the square of the difference of counts between each dimension and then taking the square root. For example, the distance between review #1 and review #2 would be calculated as

$Sqrt[(1-1)^2+(1-1)^2+(1-2)^2+(1-0)^2+(1-1)^2+(0-1)^2+(0-1)^2 ]=2.$

Table below shows the calculation of the Euclidean distance between each sentence:

**Table 3: Distance of Words**

| | Dist between review 1 and 2 in each dimension | Dist between review 1 and 3 in each dimension | Dist between review 1 and 4 in each dimension | Dist between review 2 and 3 in each dimension | Dist between review 2 and 4 in each dimension | Dist between review 3 and 4 in each dimension |
|---|---|---|---|---|---|---|
| | 0 | 0 | 1 | 0 | 1 | 1 |
| | 0 | 0 | 1 | 0 | 1 | 1 |
| | 1 | 0 | 0 | 1 | 1 | 0 |
| | 1 | 1 | 1 | 0 | 0 | 0 |
| | 0 | 0 | 0 | 1 | 0 | 1 |
| | 1 | 1 | 0 | 1 | 1 | 0 |
| | 0 | 0 | 1 | 1 | 1 | 0 |
| | 1 | 0 | 0 | 1 | 1 | 0 |
| | 1 | 1 | 0 | 1 | 0 | 0 |
| | 0 | 1 | 0 | 1 | 0 | 1 |
| | 0 | 1 | 0 | 1 | 0 | 1 |

|  | 0 | 0 | 1 | 0 | 1 | 1 |
|---|---|---|---|---|---|---|
|  | 0 | 0 | 1 | 0 | 1 | 1 |
| *Total Distance* | 2.24 | 2.24 | 2.45 | 3.00 | 3.16 | 2.65 |

*Based on this table, reviews 1, 2 and 3 are very similar since the distance between 1 and 2 is the same as that between 1 and 3 which is 2.24. But reviews 2 and 4 are very different with the distance of 3.16. If there would be no common words, the distance would be much larger and vice-versa.*

*However, when we actually look at the reviews we see that reviews 1 and 2 are similar only based on affordability but not taste, although 1 and 3 are more similar than 1 and 2.*

*So we can see that BOW doesn't work very well when there are small changes in the terminology where we have sentences with similar meaning but with just different words.*

*Due to its mechanism, we also end up with vectors with lots of zero scores called a **sparse vector**.*

***Sparse vectors** require more memory and computational resources when modeling and the vast number of positions or dimensions can make the modeling process very challenging for traditional algorithms.*

*As such, there is pressure to decrease the size of the vocabulary when using a bag-of-words model.*

*There are simple text cleaning techniques that can be used as a first step, such as:*

- *Ignoring case*
- *Ignoring punctuation*
- *Ignoring frequent words that don't contain much information, called stop words, like "a," "of," etc.*
- *Fixing misspelled words.*
- *Reducing words to their stem (e.g., "play" from "playing") using "stemming" algorithms.*

*There are other techniques such as*

1. *Tokenization: which is the process of segmenting running text into sentences and words. In essence, it's the task of cutting a text into pieces called tokens, and at the same*

*time throwing away certain characters, such as punctuation.*

2. *Stop Words Removal: which includes removing common language articles, pronouns and prepositions such as "and", "the" or "to" in English. In this process some very common words that appear to provide little or no value to the NLP objective are filtered and excluded from the text to be processed, hence removing widespread and frequent terms that are not informative about the corresponding text.*

3. *Stemming: which includes the process of slicing the end or the beginning of words with the intention of removing affixes (lexical additions to the root of the word).*

4. *Lemmatization: where the objective of reducing a word to its base form and grouping together different forms of the same word. For example, verbs in past tense are changed into present (e.g., "went" is changed to "go") and synonyms are unified (e.g. ,"best" is changed to "good"), hence standardizing words with similar meaning to their root. Although it seems closely related to the stemming process, lemmatization uses a different approach to reach the root forms of words.*

5. *Topic modeling: which is a method for uncovering hidden structures in sets of texts or documents. In essence it clusters texts to discover latent topics based on their contents, processing individual words and assigning them values based on their distribution. This technique is based on the assumptions that each document consists of a mixture of topics and that each topic consists of a set of words, which means that if we can spot these hidden topics we can unlock the meaning of our texts.*

*The different techniques shown above underscore the complexity of natural language, and the difficulty in natural language processing. If you want to learn more about NLP please refer to the following sources:*

*https://towardsdatascience.com/your-guide-to-natural-language-processing-nlp-48ea2511f6e1*

*https://monkeylearn.com/natural-language-processing/*

## Key Takeaways

- A model is defined as a process that consists of three components: (a) an information input component (b) a processing component that transforms inputs into estimates and (c) a reporting component that translates the estimates into useful information
- Linear Regression is the simplest machine learning model where the inputs and outputs have a somewhat liner relationship
- Classification problem is a type of machine learning model that reads some input and generates an output that classifies the input into some categories that are known from the beginning such as separating emails input spam or not
- Clustering is a technique that attempts to find clusters of observations within a dataset such that the observations within each cluster are quite similar to each other while observations in different clusters are quite different from each other. Different from classification, the categories are not known
- A feature is an input into the model
- Label is the output of a model in classification problems
- Natural language Processing (NLP) enables computers to understand, interpret, and generate human language.

# Chapter 4: Types of Machine Learning Models

*"No great marketing decisions have ever been made on qualitative data." – John Sculley*

Now that you have an idea of some basic machine learning models, let's dig a little deeper.

All machine learning models are typically categorized into three types as shown in Figure **11**: (a) Supervised (b) Unsupervised and (c) Reinforcement. These are described in detail below.

## Figure 11: Types of Machine Learning Models

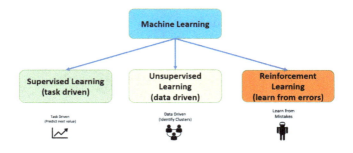

### Supervised Learning

Just like a teacher supervises the learning process, in "Supervised learning," the algorithm learns from the training dataset. Since the correct answers are known the algorithm iteratively makes predictions on the training data and is corrected by the teacher.

The examples we discussed earlier on regression and classification problems, all fall under supervised learning. Majority of practical problems like predicting probability of fraud or predicting the blood pressure based on medication dosage fall under this category.

Supervised learning is where you have input variables ($x$) such as transaction amount in the case of predicting probability of fraud or medication dosage amount in predicting blood pressure, and an output variable ($Y$) such as probability of fraud or blood pressure. You can then use an algorithm to learn the mapping function from the input to the output.

$$Y = f(x)$$

The goal is to estimate the mapping function so that when you have new input data ($x$), you can predict the output variables (Y) for that data.

Consider Figure **12** below. $x$ here would be attributes such as color = red, taste = sweet, type = fruit and $Y$, the output is Apple.

## Figure 12: Supervised Learning Example

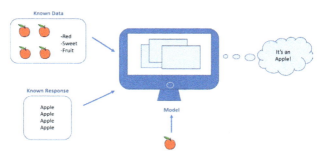

We discussed linear regression and logistic regression models that are examples of supervised learning.

Another type of models used in supervised learning are decision tree based models described in Chapter 5.

### Unsupervised Learning

Unsupervised learning is where you only have input data ($x$) and no corresponding output variables.

Unsupervised learning uses machine learning algorithms to analyze and cluster unlabeled datasets like the clustering algorithm discussed in the previous chapter. **These algorithms discover hidden patterns or data groupings without the need for human intervention.**

These are called unsupervised learning because unlike supervised learning above there is no correct answer and there is no teacher. Algorithms are left to their own devices to discover and present the interesting structure in the data.

Unsupervised learning problems can be further grouped into clustering and association problems.

Clustering: A clustering problem is where you want to discover the inherent groupings in the data, such as grouping customers by purchasing behavior.

**Figure 13: Unsupervised Learning Example**

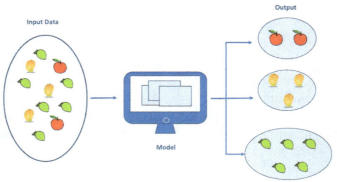

Practical examples of unsupervised learning include (as discussed in the previous chapter): Customer segmentation (differentiating groups of customers based on some attributes), Anomaly detection (for example, to detect bot activity) and Pattern recognition (grouping images, transcribing audio etc.).

Association: An association rule learning problem is where you want to discover rules that describe large portions of your data, such as people that buy a new home also tend to buy new furniture. This is used by online retail companies like Amazon and Walmart to suggest additional products that a customer may be interested in based on their purchase history.

## Figure 14: Association Machine Learning Example

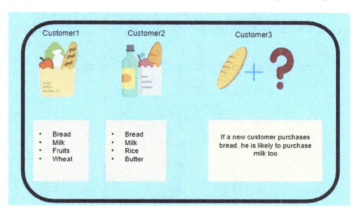

### Reinforcement Learning

Reinforcement learning is the training of machine learning models to make a sequence of decisions. In reinforcement learning, developers devise a method of rewarding desired behaviors and punishing negative behaviors (see Figure **15**).

## Figure 15: Reinforcement Learning Example

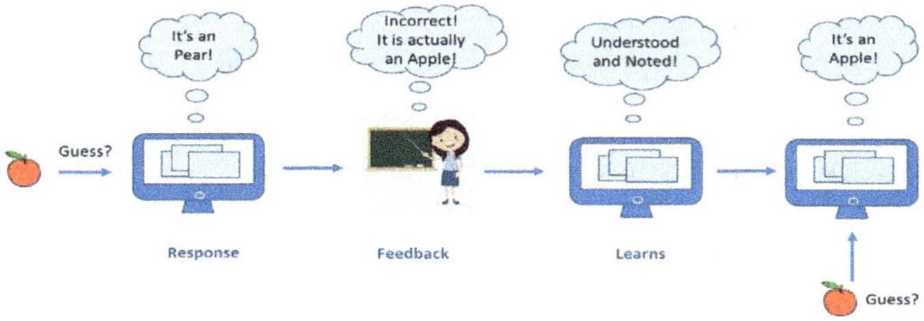

Practical examples of reinforcement learning include self-driving cars where the cars make a decision about when to stop, turn or go and customized actions in video games such as Mario.

The key components of Reinforcement Learning and how each component interacts with other components are described below (see Figure **16**).

## Figure 16: Components of Reinforcement Learning

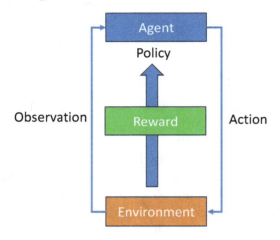

Agent: it can be a game character, robot, or car. An agent is an algorithm that takes an action. In real life the agent is a human.

Action: is a set of all possible moves that an agent can perform. For example, Mario can jump, move left, right, and duck.

Environment: it is a world that interacts with agents. In Mario, the environment is the map. It takes the current state and agent's action as an input and returns the reward and the next state.

Reward: is feedback or a prize given to an agent based on the previous action. It can be positive if the agent has completed the task and negative if it fails. Rewards can also be immediate and delayed.

Policy: is a strategy that agents employees to get the highest possible rewards based on state and action. In simple words, it defines how an agent will take action based on the current state.

Observation: Observation is the information that the agent is gathering from the environment.

A great resource to Reinforcement Learning can be found at https://cars.stanford.edu/video/tutorial-reinforcement-learning

**Key Takeaways**

The three types of machine learning models are:

- Supervised Learning where algorithm learns from the training dataset e.g., regression, classification
- Unsupervised Learning is where you have input data and no corresponding output variables for each input data variable. Algorithms discover hidden patterns or data groupings without the need for human intervention such as clustering
- Reinforcement Learning is the training of machine learning models to make a sequence of decisions such as algorithm used in driverless cars

# Chapter 5: Tree Based Models

*"Big branches in the decision tree require extra caution. These are the forks in the road that leave us with no way back." -- Garry Kasparov*

Tree-based models use a series of "if-then" rules to generate predictions from one or more decision trees. These models can be used for either regression (predicting numerical values) or classification (predicting categorical values).

Three types of commonly used tree-based models are:

- Decision tree models, which are the foundation of all tree-based models.
- Random forest models, an "ensemble" method which builds many decision trees in parallel.
- Gradient boosting models, an "ensemble" method which builds many decision trees sequentially.

### Decision Tree Models

First, let's start with a simple decision tree. A decision tree can be used to visually represent the "decisions", or if-then rules, that are used to generate predictions. Let us consider an example where, depending on the weather outlook, you need to decide whether to play tennis or not. If it is rainy, you can clearly not play if you only have access to outdoor courts. If it is sunny, you may not want to play if the temperature is too high (say your threshold is 90F). Your decision tree may look something like the figure shown below.

**Figure 17: Simple Decision Tree**

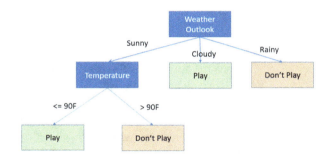

A decision tree goes through each decision node or a yes or no question, in the tree and will move down the tree accordingly, until the final predictions. The first question, where we are looking at the range of weather options, is called the root node. The final nodes with decisions are called leaf nodes or terminal nodes. The intermediate nodes are called decision nodes. The branches extending from a decision node are decision branches, each branch representing one of the possible alternatives or courses of action available at that point.

Here, we're trying to predict whether to play tennis or not, hence it is an example of a classification tree. Trees can be easily converted into a regression tree by predicting an actual numerical value based on certain other factors.

### *Optional: Using Decision Trees for Regression and Classification*

*Below I have described how one might develop a decision tree model for regression and another one for classification.*

*For regression, I chose an example where the input dataset containing an independent variable x and a dependent variable y does not seem to have any obvious pattern such as a linear relationship. For example, grade point average vs age of the student.*

*For the classification problem I chose a hypothetical example of a scatter plot of red and blue dots for given values of x and y. The problem you want to solve is for a particular value of x and y, what should be the appropriate color of the dot.*

*Decision Trees for Regression Models*

*Let us consider a dataset with 2 variables shown below and the associated figure for which we want to develop a decision tree model to predict the value for y given a value for x just like we did for linear regression.*

## Table 4: Input Dataset for Regression

| Points | x | y |
|--------|-----|-----|
| 1 | 1 | 1 |
| 2 | 2 | 1.2 |
| 3 | 3 | 1.4 |
| 4 | 4 | 1.1 |
| 5 | 5 | 1 |
| 6 | 6 | 5.5 |
| 7 | 7 | 6.1 |
| 8 | 8 | 6.7 |
| 9 | 9 | 6.4 |
| 10 | 10 | 6 |
| 11 | 11 | 6 |
| 12 | 12 | 3 |
| 13 | 13 | 3.2 |
| 14 | 14 | 3.1 |

## Figure 18: Input Data for Decision Tree

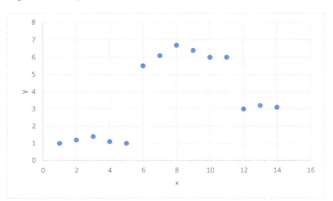

To develop a decision tree model to predict a value of y for a given value of x we follow these steps:

*Step 1*

*The first step is to sort the data based on x (in this case, it is already sorted ). Then, take the average of the first 2 rows in variable x ( which is (1+2)/2 = 1.5 according to the given dataset ). Then divide the dataset into 2 parts ( Part A and Part B ) , separated by x < 1.5 and x ≥ 1.5 (basically create 2 branches at the root node of x=1.5.*

*Now, Part A consists only of one point, which is the first row (1,1) and all the other points are in Part B. Now, take the average of all the y values in Part A and average of all y values in Part B separately. These 2 values are the predicted output of the decision tree for x < 1.5 and x ≥ 1.5 respectively. Using the predicted and original values, calculate the mean square error using the formula below and note it down.*

$$Mean\ squared\ error = \frac{1}{n}\sum_{i=1}^{n}(predicted_i - yactual_i)^2$$

*Step 2*

*In step 1, we calculated the average for the first 2 numbers of sorted x and split the dataset based on that and calculated the predictions. Then, we do the same process again but this time, we calculate the average for the second 2 numbers of sorted x ( (2+3)/2 = 2.5 ). Then, we split the dataset again based on x < 2.5 and x ≥ 2.5 into Part A and Part B again and predict outputs, find mean square error as shown in step 1. This process is repeated for the third 2 numbers, the fourth 2 numbers, the 5th, 6th, 7th till n-1th 2 numbers (where n is the number of records or rows in the dataset , in this case 14).*

*Step 3*

*Now that we have n-1 mean squared errors calculated, we need to choose the point at which we are going to split the dataset. And that point is the point, which resulted in the lowest mean squared error on splitting at it. In this case, the point turns out to be at x=5.5.*

*Hence the tree will be split into 2 parts. x<5.5 and x≥ 5.5. The root node is selected this way and the data points that go* *towards the left child and right child of the root node are further recursively exposed to the same algorithm for further splitting.*

*The resulting decision tree and the splits on the graph look like*

**Figure 19: Regression Decision Tree Output**

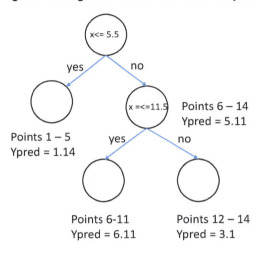

**Figure 20: Regression Decision Tree Output**

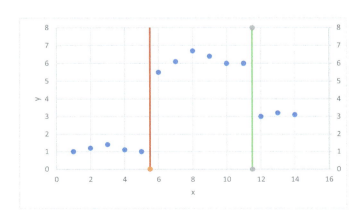

*Then if you want to predict the value of y for a given value of x, you just traverse down the tree until you reach the terminal node and simply take the average of all known values of y at that node. For example, if you want to predict the value of y for x = 12.5, the predicted value of y would be an average of all y values of points 12-14 which will be 3.1.*

*In Chapter 4, we discussed using a linear regression model to try to predict blood pressure using independent variables such as height, weight, age, gender, and hours of exercise per week. Using decision trees can achieve the same goal but decision tree approach may be a little more predictive if the data points do not follow a simple linear pattern. Thus when the data points follow a somewhat linear pattern, linear regression method is preferable, where as if the data does not follow a simple pattern such as depicted in the example here, a decision tree approach is preferable.*

*Decision Trees for Classification Models*

*Decision trees can also be used for classification as mentioned earlier.*

*Let's take an example of a dataset shown below along with the associated figure.*

## *Table 5: Input Dataset for Classification*

| | Red dots | | | Blue Dots | |
|---|---|---|---|---|---|
| x | y | | | x | y |
| -20 | 0 | | | -7 | -5 |
| -17 | -5 | | | -6 | 6 |
| -16 | 5 | | | -4 | 4 |
| -5 | 20 | | | 0 | 0 |
| -12 | -12 | | | 2 | 8 |
| 25 | -5 | | | 2 | -6 |
| 9 | 14 | | | 4 | -5 |
| 12 | 12 | | | 7 | 0 |
| 17 | 0 | | | 8 | -6 |
| 18 | -6 | | | 9 | 4 |

*We have red and blue dots scattered based on the x (horizontal axis) and y (vertical axis) axis (see*

*Figure* 21).

The way to solve for classification problems is very similar to that for regression, except the predicted values for each node is the probability for belonging to that class.

For regression model, we minimized the mean square error but for classification we maximize something called information gain. Before I describe information gain, let us look at the concept of something called entropy defined as

$$Entropy = \sum_{i=1}^{n} \left(-p_i \, log \, (p_i)\right)$$

Where $p_i$ is the probability of being in a particular class at a node and n is equal to the number of classes in this case 2 (red and blue).

**Figure 21: Classification Decision Tree Output**

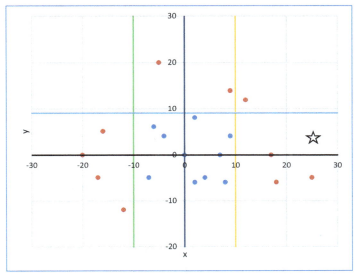

Let us look at a possible decision tree as depicted below. We see that all leaf or terminal nodes are pure meaning they all belong to one class only. So how do we determine the decision points for x and y?

**Figure 22: Classification Decision Tree Output**

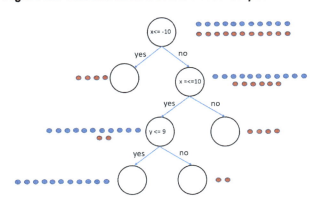

*We start by calculating the entropy at root node which is equal to*

$Entropy = -0.5 * log(.5) - 0.5 * log(0.5) = 1$

*The probability of a red (and blue) dot at the root note = 0.5 since we have an equal number of red and blue dots.*

*Similarly, the entropy at top 1st left decision node = 0 since we only have red dots. Entropy at 1st right decision node = -6/17\*log(6/17)-11/17\*log(11/17) = 0.28 since we have 6 red dots and 11 blue dots and so on.*

*Then we calculate something called information gain which is equal to the entropy at the root node minus the sum of entropies at all child nodes.*

*Just like we minimized the mean squared error for regression, here we iteratively solve for splits by maximizing gain.*

*The green line in the figure represents x = -10, the yellow line represents x = 10 and the blue line represents y = 9.*

*Now let's say you want to predict the class for input values for x and y as 15 and 7 respectively (shown as a star on the plot) and you want to predict whether that point will be categorized as a blue or red dot. Following the decision tree, from the root node, we go to the right since x > -10. On the 2nd node, x is > 10, so we again traverse right and end up with red. Hence that point will be classified as red.*

*There are essentially two key components to building a decision tree model whether it is classification or regression: determining which features/variables to split on and then deciding when to stop splitting.*

*Understanding basic decision trees are a foundation for tree based machine learning algorithms explained later.*

*For more information on techniques on features to split on, when to stop splitting etc., several resources are available, such as:*

*https://medium.com/analytics-vidhya/regression-trees-decision-tree-for-regression-machine-learning-e4d7525d8047 https://www.analyticssteps.com/blogs/classification-and-regression-tree-cart-algorithm*

### Ensemble Methods

Note that a single decision tree model will generally not produce strong predictions since it may lead to over-fitting, which means that the model works really well for the data points in the training set but does not fit that well on the data the model has never seen, also called "testing set."

To improve our model's predictive power, one can build many trees and combine the predictions, which is called *ensembling*. Ensembling actually refers to any combination of models, but is most frequently used to refer to tree-based models.

A good example of why ensemble methods are powerful is described below.

Let's say you are looking for a good movie to watch on a Saturday evening.

**Option 1**: Look for reviews of movies from your favorite newspaper such as the New York Times or the Wall Street Journal

**Option 2**: Use Google and randomly look at one user's review for a couple of movies

**Option 3**: Use International Movie Database (IMDB) and look at the average ratings ensuring the number of people who have rated the movie is in the thousands.

Let us analyze each of the above-mentioned solutions.

**Option 1:**

Movie critics are in general accurate. However, your movie preference might not be aligned with the critic's choices.

**Option 2:**

A random person's star rating for a movie on the internet is easier to find but again may not be aligned with your liking and solution could be biased.

**Option 3:**

Collectively it might be just the right amount of accuracy you need and easier to find over the internet. It is much less biased, since the users who have rated the movies come from various backgrounds.

Hence without the need to look for a recommendation from a movie critic, you can get a reasonably good recommendation on movies just by looking at a collective opinion of a group of random (but large) people.

The idea for ensemble models is that by combining output from many different models, you come up with a final model that is much more accurate.

Ensembling technique is used frequently in applications such as fraud prediction. Instead of relying on a single model, you build several models either using different features or using different techniques or both and combine the results together which is likely to give you better outcome.

Two of the most popular ensemble algorithms are *random forest* and *gradient boosting*, which are quite powerful and commonly used for advanced machine learning applications.

Random forest models are a group of decision tree models trained on different subsets of the dataset, and the final output is generated by collating the outputs of all the different models.

Boosting is an ensemble tree method that builds consecutive small trees — often only one node — with each tree focused on correcting the net error from the previous tree. So, we split our first tree on the most predictive feature and then update weights to ensure that the subsequent tree splits on whichever feature allows it to correctly classify the data points that were misclassified in the initial tree. The next tree will then focus on correctly classifying errors from that tree, and so on. The final prediction is a weighted sum of all individual predictions.

You can learn more about random forest and gradient boosting by going to the following resources:

https://towardsdatascience.com/understanding-random-forest-58381e0602d2

https://towardsdatascience.com/all-you-need-to-know-about-gradient-boosting-algorithm-part-1-regression-2520a34a502

## Key Takeaways

- Tree-based models are very popular in machine learning.
- The decision tree model, the foundation of tree-based models, is quite straightforward to interpret, but generally is not a very strong model.
- Ensemble models can be used to generate stronger predictions from many trees, with random forest and gradient boosting as two of the most popular.
- All tree-based models can be used for regression or classification and can handle non-linear relationships quite well

.

# Chapter 6: Artificial Neural Networks

*"I think the brain is essentially a computer and consciousness is like a computer program. It will cease to run when the computer is turned off. Theoretically, it could be re-created on a neural network, but that would be very difficult, as it would require all one's memories".*
*–Stephen Hawking*

As mentioned briefly in Chapter 2, Deep Learning is a subset of ML, which uses artificial neural networks or ANNs that attempt to simulate the behavior of the human brain allowing it to "learn" from large amounts of data.

The human brain consists of about 12 billion nerve cells or neurons[4] and each neuron is, on average, connected to several thousand other neurons. Neurons communicate via a combination of electrical and chemical signals. Within the neuron, electrical signals driven by charged particles allow rapid conduction from one end of the cell to the other.

One very important feature of neurons is that they do not react immediately to the reception of signals or energy. Instead, they sum their received

---

[4]

https://thebrain.mcgill.ca/flash/d/d_07/d_07_cl/d_0
7_cl_tra/d_07_cl_tra.html

energies, and they send their own quantities of energy to other neurons only when this sum has reached a certain critical threshold. The brain learns by adjusting the number and strength of these connections.

See the schematic of two neurons in the figure below. Each neuron has one long cable that snakes away from the main part of the cell. This cable, several times thinner than a human hair, is called an axon, and it is where electrical impulses from the neuron travel away to be received by other neurons. The places where neurons connect and communicate with each other are called synapses. Even though this picture is a simplification of the biological facts, it is sufficiently powerful to serve as a model for the neural net.

**Figure 23: Schematic of Two Neurons**[5]

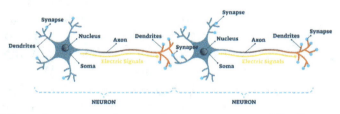

Neural networks—and more specifically, artificial neural networks (ANNs)—mimic the human brain through a set of algorithms.

See figure below for schematic of an ANN. The circles represent neurons and arrows that connect each neuron to another are like axons and synapses.

---

[5] https://www.simplypsychology.org/neuron.html

### Figure 24: Artificial Neural Network

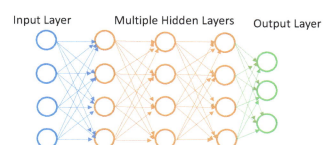

Input Layer    Multiple Hidden Layers    Output Layer

The input layer of a neural network is composed of artificial input neurons, which brings the initial data into the system for further processing by subsequent layers of artificial neurons. The input layer is the very beginning of the workflow for the artificial neural network.

Hidden layers allow for the function of a neural network to be broken down into specific transformations of the data. In human neural networks, these are the networks of cells where neurons communicate with one another at synapses.

The output layer is the final layer in the neural network where desired predictions are obtained. This is similar to the brain recognizing the image of a cat or a dog. The outer layer depends on the activity of the preceding hidden layers. Just like in human neural networks, if there is a misfiring, the output may not be reliable.

#### *Optional: Neural Network Math Basics*

*At a basic level, a neural network is comprised of four main components: inputs, weights, a bias or threshold, and an output. Similar to linear regression, the algebraic formula would look something like this:*

$$\sum_{j=0}^{n} w_j x_j + bias = w_1 x_1 + w_2 x_2 + w_3 x_3 + + bias$$

*Where w is the weight, x is the input and n is the number of neurons in a layer.*

*To understand this in simpler terms, let us apply it to a more tangible example, like whether or not you should order a pizza for dinner (see Figure 25). This will be our predicted outcome, or ŷ. Let's assume that there are three main factors that will influence your decision:*

- $x_1$ = *If you will save time by ordering out (Yes: 1; No: 0)*
- $x_2$ = *If you will lose weight by ordering a pizza (Yes: 1; No: 0)*
- $x_3$ = *If you will save money (Yes: 1; No: 0)*

### Figure 25: Simple neural network for pizza ordering determination

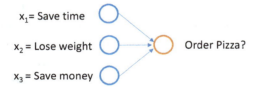

*Then, let's assume the following, giving us the following inputs:*

- $x_1$ = *1, since you're not making dinner*
- $x_2$ = *0, since we're getting ALL the toppings*
- $x_3$ = *1, since we're only getting 2 slices*

*For simplicity purposes, our inputs will have a binary value of 0 or 1. We now need to assign some weights to determine the importance of these factors. Larger weights make a single input's contribution to the output more significant compared to other inputs.*

- $w_1$ = 5, highest weight since you value time
- $w_2$ = 3, slightly lower weight since you value staying in shape
- $w_3$ = 2, least weight since you've got money in the bank but you still want to consider

Finally, we'll also assume a threshold value of 5, which would translate to a bias value of –5.

Since we established all the relevant values for our summation, we can now plug them into this formula.

$$\sum_{j=0}^{n} w_j x_j + bias = w_1 x_1 + w_2 x_2 + w_3 x_3 + +bias$$

Using the following activation function, we can now calculate the output (i.e., our decision to order pizza):

$$output = \hat{y} = f(x) = \begin{cases} 1, & if \sum w_j x_j + bias \geq 0 \\ 0, & if \sum w_j x_j + bias < 0 \end{cases}$$

In summary:

$\hat{y}$ (our predicted outcome) = Decide to order pizza or not

$\hat{y}$ = (1*5) + (0*3) + (1*2) - 5

$\hat{y}$ = 5 + 0 + 2 – 5

$\hat{y}$ = 2, which is greater than zero.

Since $\hat{y}$ is 2, the output from the activation function will be 1, meaning that we will order pizza. Yayy! Next decision: To beer or not to beer.

Applying this example to the ANN then, if the output of any individual node is above the specified threshold value, that node is activated, sending data to the next layer of the network just like an actual neuron. Otherwise, no data is passed along to the next layer of the network.

Now, imagine the above process being repeated multiple times for a single decision through multiple "hidden" layers as part of deep learning algorithms. Each hidden layer has its own activation function, potentially passing information from the *previous layer into the next one. Once all the outputs from the hidden layers are generated, then they are used as inputs to calculate the final output of the neural network. Again, the above example is just the most basic example of a neural network; most real-world examples are nonlinear and far more complex.*

An ANN can have one or many hidden layers, depending on the complexity of the problem it is designed to solve. When an ANN has multiple hidden layers, it is commonly referred to as a deep neural network (DNN).

A DNN is called a Feed Forward Neural Network (FFNNs) when data flows from the input layer to the output layer without going backward and the links between the layers are one way which is in the forward direction and they never touch a node again. **Figure 24** shows an FFNN since all arrows are pointing forward.

There are several types of DNN models. The most common ones are described below:

### Recurrent Neural Network (RNN)

A Recurrent Neural Network (RNN) is an FFNN with a time component. This neural network has connections between passes and connections through time, meaning, connections between nodes allows information to flow back into the previous parts of the network so that each model in the layers depends on past events, allowing information to persist (see

**Figure 26** below). The most common application is in time series.

In time series data, the current observation depends on previous observations. Thus, observations are not independent from each other. Traditional neural networks, however, view each observation as independent, because the networks are not able to retain past or historical information. Basically, they have no memory of what happened in the past. (Like in the movie "Groundhog Day" where Phil has no recollection of what happened the previous day and keeps reliving the same day over and over

Past information is sometimes key to solving some problems, e.g., predicting fraud based on past payment behavior. These situations led to the rise of Recurrent Neural Networks (RNNs), which introduce the concept of memory to neural networks by including the dependency between data points. With this, RNNs can be trained to remember concepts based on context, i.e., learn repeated patterns. RNNs are ideal for sequential data such as text, time series, financial data, speech, audio etc. where sequence is more important than the individual items themselves.

## Figure 26: Recurrent Neural Network

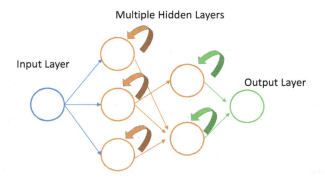

### Convolutional Neural Network (CNN)

Before going into CNNs, let's look at a practical application of ANNs, namely image classification. Image classification is the process of taking an input (like a picture) and outputting a class (like "cat") or a probability that the input is a particular class ("there's a 90% probability that this input is a cat"). For humans it seems very natural since as our brains develop, we consume inordinate amounts of data and we learn based on what we are taught at home, in school or from books. But how does a computer do it? This is where a CNN comes in.

The architecture of a CNN is analogous to that of the connectivity pattern of Neurons in the Human Brain and was inspired by the organization of the Visual Cortex. Individual neurons respond to stimuli only in a restricted region of the visual field known as the Receptive Field. A collection of such fields overlap to cover the entire visual area. Thus RNN can be considered as helping in data processing to predict our next step. CNN on the other hand, can be considered as helping in the analysis of images.

A CNN works by extracting features from images. A convolution (a simple application of a filter to an input that results in an activation) is essentially sliding a filter over the input. In simpler words, each neuron works in its receptive field and is later connected to other neurons in the network in a way that covers the entire visual field (see figure below). After convolution, pooling occurs. The purpose of the pooling layers is to reduce the dimensions of the hidden layer. It does this by combining the outputs of neuron clusters at the previous layer into a single neuron in the next layer.

**Figure 27: Convolutional Neural Network**

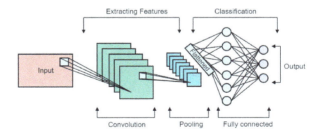

This eliminates the need for manual feature extraction meaning a human determining the features that are most important in training the model. The features are not trained! They're learned while the network trains on a set of images. This makes deep learning models extremely accurate for computer vision tasks. CNNs learn feature detection through tens or hundreds of hidden layers. Each layer increases the complexity of the learned features.

Although CNN is a very powerful technique for image classification, there are risks associated as well. There is a somewhat famous story in AI research circles about a neural network model that was trained to distinguish between wolves and huskies. The model learned to identify them successfully, achieving high accuracy when given images that weren't used for its training, i.e. testing set.

However, it soon became apparent some very clear images were being misclassified. When they looked into why the neural network was making such gross mistakes, researchers figured out the model learned to classify an image based on whether there was snow in it — all images of wolves used in the training had snow in the background, while the ones of huskies did not. Unsurprisingly, the model was failing.

Hence, before relying on a model, it is important to test it comprehensively for all inputs prior to making decisions based on outcomes.

If you are interested in learning more about the different types of neural networks, here are some very useful sites:

https://www.analyticsvidhya.com/blog/2020/02/cnn-vs-rnn-vs-mlp-analyzing-3-types-of-neural-networks-in-deep-learning/

https://www.knowledgehut.com/blog/data-science/types-of-neural-networks

## Key Takeaways

- Artificial Neural Networks (ANN) mimic the human brain through a set of algorithms.
- A neural network has three types of layers:
  - Input layer brings the initial data into the system and is the beginning of the workflow
  - Hidden layers allow for the function of a neural network to be broken down into specific transformations of the data like synapses in humans
  - Output layer is the final layer where desired predictions are obtained
- If an ANN has multiple hidden layers it is called a deep neural network (DNN)
- Recurrent Neural Network (RNN) has a time component where nodes allow information to flow back into the previous parts of the network and ideal for sequential data, time series, speech, audio etc.
- Convolutional Neural Network (CNN) works by extracting features from images and is analogous to that of the connectivity pattern of neurons in the human brain

# Chapter 7: AI/ML Model Risks

*"By far, the greatest danger of Artificial Intelligence*
*is that people conclude too early that they understand it"*
*– Eliezer Yudkowsky*

Before handing over important decision-making to a computer model, it is important to ensure its safety and reliability. In other words, how do we manage the risks of AI/ML models? The first step, of course, is to identify where the risks arise in the model. You may have also heard about "hallucinations". Hallucination is the term employed for the phenomenon where AI algorithms and deep learning neural networks produce outputs that are not real, do not match any data the algorithm has been trained on, or any other identifiable pattern.

Consider the following example of AI making incorrect recommendations from seemingly correct inputs. Mary is planning her daughter's wedding and has been conducting online searches for wedding venues, caterers, flower vendors etc. Her mother is turning eighty and Mary has also been looking for anti-aging products at her mother's request. An algorithm picks Mary's searches and concludes that Mary is likely an older person who is getting married. It starts sending Mary information about mature brides! You get the idea!

So let's dive in to see where these types of risks can arise.

Figure below shows the different components of model risk. Each area is described in detail below with examples.

**Figure 28: Components of Model Risk**

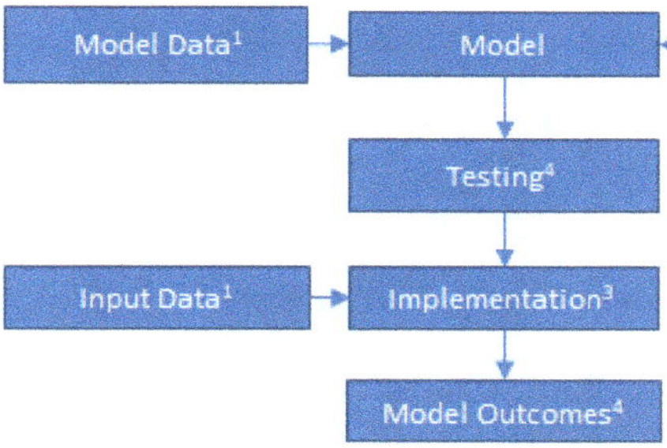

### Model Data Risk

Model Data risk is defined as the possibility that either the data used to develop the model or the data that is used as an input to the model at run time ("production data") are inappropriate, incomplete, or inaccurate.

It can arise from a number of sources including the following:

– Using proxy data, such as the data from a different portfolio or even a different institution, to develop the model when the desired data are not available.

*Example: You want to analyze the population of Indianapolis but the only data available is of Boston. Using Boston may lead to errors since the Boston data is not representative of Indianapolis data*

## Table 6: Total Population by Age in 2022

**Est. Total Population By Age**

| | Boston, MA | Indianapolis, IN |
|---|---|---|
| Age 0 to 4 | 5.2% | 7.4% |
| Age 5 to 9 | 4.3% | 6.9% |
| Age 10 to 14 | 4.1% | 6.6% |
| Age 15 to 17 | 2.7% | 3.8% |
| Age 18 to 20 | 7.1% | 3.8% |
| Age 21 to 24 | 8.3% | 6.1% |
| Age 25 to 34 | 23.8% | 16.7% |
| Age 35 to 44 | 12.5% | 12.9% |
| Age 45 to 54 | 11.1% | 12.6% |
| Age 55 to 59 | 5.3% | 6.4% |
| Age 60 to 64 | 4.6% | 5.4% |
| Age 65 to 74 | 6.2% | 6.6% |
| Age 75 to 84 | 3.2% | 3.4% |

– Using outdated data that is not representative of the current portfolio to develop the model.

*Example: You want to analyze the population of Boston today but the data available is ten years old*

## Table 7: Historical Population Distribution of Boston

|  | Boston, MA |
|---|---|
| Population | 691,531 |
| Female Population | 51.9% |
| Male Population | 48.1% |
| Median Age | 32 |
|  |  |
| Population - 2010 | 621.053 |
| Population - 2000 | 589,141 |
| Population - 1990 | 574,283 |
| Pop. 2000 to Now | 17.4% |
| Pop. 1990 to Now | 20.4% |

– Extracting data from the wrong internal data source, or misunderstanding the definitions of the extracted data fields

*Example: When developing a model for auto loan default, using the field of origination FICO score when you actually want current FICO score*

– Biased data due to developer exclusions or design of data sample

*Example 1: A sophisticated image recognition algorithm has been built to identify shoes but the development dataset only contained athletic shoes. The model will not recognize high heels as shoes*

**Figure 29: Images of Shoes**

*Example 2: You want to find correlation between unemployment rate and stock index but do not consider the full economic cycle. Instead, you only focus on the time period when they were positively correlated*

**Figure 30: Wilshire 5000 Total Market Full Cap Index vs Unemployment Rate**

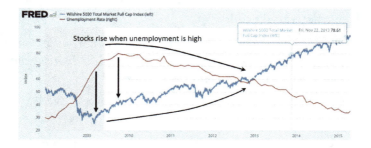

**Model Theory Risk**

Model Theory risk is defined as the possibility of using inappropriate methodology or assumptions, or model misspecification. It can manifest itself in many ways, including (but not limited to):

– Choosing a model development approach that is not suitable for the business problem at hand

*Example: Choosing a deep neural network methodology for credit scoring with no capability to give decline reasons. This could result in non-compliance with regulations such as Consumer Financial Protection Bureau's Regulation B (Equal Credit Opportunity Act)*

– Choosing a statistical estimation technique that is not appropriate for the business problem or the available development data

*Example: Using linear regression instead of logistic regression for calculating the probability of default. Probability of default lies between 0 and 1 with a probability higher than 0.5 representing "yes." Using linear regression may result in calculated probabilities outside of the range of 0 and 1.*

– Using input variables that do not have logical business relationships with the dependent variable, omitting important variables from the model, or including multiple highly correlated independent variables

*Example: You look at the relationship between ice cream sales and shark attacks and assume that as shark attacks increase, the ice cream sales are expected to increase whereas both these have a similar trend due to the*

*time of the year. You may apply this model when ordering ice cream for your business and be completely off since this model is incorrect!*

**Figure 31: Ice cream Sales and Shark Attacks**

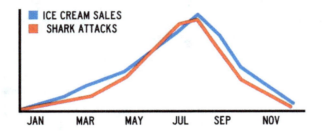

– Over-fitting the model to development data

*Example: Model performs extremely well in development dataset but poorly on out of sample data that the model has never seen before. This happens quite frequently in financial forecasting where managers scratch their heads when the forecast is completely off!*

**Figure 32: Underfitting and Overfitting**

## Model Implementation Risk

Model Implementation risk is defined as the possibility that the production implementation of the model is mathematically inaccurate or inconsistent or does not perform like it did in the development environment due to the complexity of the application.

You might recall the rollout of Obamacare when it was initially launched[6]. The biggest contractor, CGI Federal, was awarded its $94 million contract in December 2011. But the government was so slow in issuing specifications that the firm did not start writing software code until spring of 2013, according to people familiar with the process. The result was two weeks after the rollout, a system costing more than $400 million and billed as a one-stop click-and-go hub for citizens seeking health insurance had thwarted the efforts of millions to simply log in. The system was not deployed or implemented by conducting sufficient testing.

### Model Outcomes & Uncertainty Risk

The Model Outcomes and Uncertainty Risk reflects the possibility that model outputs are biased, lack acceptable predictive power, or are subject to a great degree of uncertainty. To determine the risk posed by a given model, we carefully consider the characteristics of the model as well as any known information about its performance, including the following factors:

---

[6] https://www.nytimes.com/2013/10/13/us/politics/from-the-start-signs-of-trouble-at-health-portal.html

- Whether the model can be back-tested (or how good your model was in predicting something based on what actually happened)

    *Example: A model used to calculate the fraud probability had an ROC[7] of 0.6 which is just slightly better than a random classifier.*

### Model Governance and Use Risk

Model Governance and Misuse risk category covers three distinct types of risks that are associated with the post-implementation use of the model:

- The risk that the model outputs or the model itself will be misused by the users

    *Example: The developers built a fraud model using data from US but the users are applying the model for predicting fraud probability in Europe*

- The risk that an operational error including the use of incorrect setting and assumptions produce erroneous results

- The risk that change management and version controls is not followed

    This chapter gave an introduction to the different types of risks that can arise from using these models. The next chapter goes into detail on bias that can arise from using these types of models.

---

[7] ROC stands for Receiver Operating Characteristic curve explained in chapter 3 and is often used in gauging the effectiveness of classification problems.

## Key Takeaways

Components of Model Risk are
- Data Risk: Risk that the data used to build the model is inaccurate, inappropriate or incomplete
- Theory Risk: Risk that an inappropriate methodology or assumptions or model specification is use
- Implementation Risk: Risk that the production implementation of the model is inaccurate or inconsistent compared to development environment
- Outcome Risk: Risk that the model results are biased, lack acceptable predictive power, or are subject to a great degree of uncertainty
- Governance and Use risk: Risk that outputs will be misused by users, model has operational errors e.g. incorrect settings, change management process not followed

# Chapter 8: Model Bias Sources

*"We need the ability to not only have high-performance models, but also to understand when we cannot trust those models." – Alexander Amini*

The previous chapters covered the different machine learning models and associated risks.

Since the machine learning models use tremendous amounts of data and some of the more sophisticated models are not as easy to explain or interpret, it is important to know that they can be a source of bias.

One of the most comprehensive papers related to bias in AI models is by Harini Suresh and John Guttag called *"Understanding Potential Sources of Harm throughout the Machine Learning Life Cycle"*. In this case study, the authors provided a framework that identifies seven distinct potential sources of downstream harm in machine learning, spanning data collection, development, and deployment. They describe how these issues arise, how they are relevant to particular applications, and how they motivate different mitigations.

As was discussed in the earlier chapters, all machine learning models start with collecting and preparing the model development data, followed by the use of an algorithm for model theory and implementing the model. The last chapter discussed the risks associated with all models including

AI/ML models. In addition to the risks, all these could also be sources of bias and are discussed below with example

### Historical Bias

Historical bias arises even if data is perfectly measured and sampled, because the historical data that was collected may be the result of bias in when the data repositories themselves were created.

For example, consider an AI system trained on some data to determine potential customers based on their ability to afford certain goods and services.

Women, as a whole, face "gender pay gap," barriers (see Figure 33) to leadership roles in the workplace, and experience reduced employment opportunities due to family and caring responsibilities. These structural issues mean women are less likely to earn as much as men. If an individual's income is an important factor in determining their suitability as a customer of a particular service, an AI system tasked with selecting future customers would likely exhibit preferential treatment towards men.

When the AI system is trained using historical data, the system will likely reject more women as potential customers.

## Figure 33: Gender Pay Gap

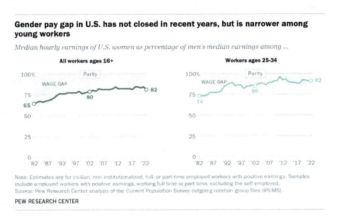

**Gender pay gap in U.S. has not closed in recent years, but is narrower among young workers**

*Median hourly earnings of U.S. women as percentage of men's median earnings among ...*

Note: Estimates are for civilian, non-institutionalized, full- or part-time employed workers with positive earnings. Samples include employed workers with positive earnings, working full time or part time, excluding the self employed.
Source: Pew Research Center analysis of the Current Population Survey outgoing rotation group files (IPUMS).

PEW RESEARCH CENTER

## Representation Bias

Representation bias occurs when the development data does not represent some part of the population adequately when the model is applied to. As a result, when the model is applied to that population, it performs unsatisfactorily.

For example, ImageNet is a widely used image dataset consisting of 1.2 million labeled images. However, ImageNet does not evenly sample from a wide population; instead, approximately 45 percent of the images in ImageNet were taken in the United States, and the majority of the remaining images are from North America or Western Europe. Only 1 percent and 2.1 percent of the images were from China and India respectively. Although ImageNet is intended to be used everywhere, some researchers[8] demonstrated that the performance on models

---

8

https://static.googleusercontent.com/media/research.google.com/en//pubs/archive/210f9d77c87f8cc471790358f69b4970a8e767ef.pdf

trained on this data performed significantly worse at classifying images such as bride or groom when the images came from undersampled countries such as India or Pakistan.

**Figure 34: Images of Newly-Weds**

### Measurement Bias

Measurement bias occurs when choosing, collecting, or computing features and labels to use in a prediction problem. Typically, a feature or label is a proxy chosen to approximate some construct (an idea or concept) that is not directly encoded or observable. For example, consider factory workers at several different locations who are monitored to count the number of errors that occur (i.e., the observed number of errors is being used as a proxy for work quality). If one location is monitored much more stringently or frequently, there will be more errors observed for that group. This can also lead to a feedback loop wherein the group is subject to further monitoring because of the apparent higher rate of mistakes.

**Figure 35: Sources of Bias in Machine Learning Models**

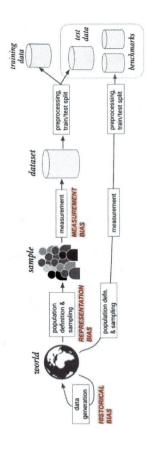
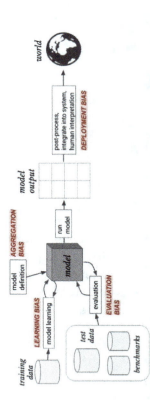

## Aggregation Bias

Aggregation bias arises when a one-size-fits-all model is used for data in which there are underlying groups or types of examples that should be considered differently. Underlying aggregation bias is an assumption that the mapping from inputs to labels is consistent across subsets of the data. For example, say a machine learning model is developed to predict and aid in diagnosing diabetes patients. Research[9] has shown that South Asians are more predisposed to diabetes than other populations all else being equal. If ethnicity is not incorporated as a feature in the data, the model may not perform well on this specific population.

### Figure 36: BMI vs Diabetes Prevalence9

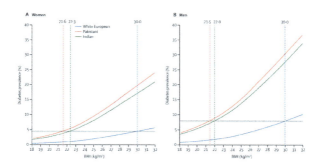

---

[9] https://www.ncbi.nlm.nih.gov/pmc/articles/PMC4026332/
https://www.thelancet.com/journals/landia/article/PIIS2213-8587%2815%2900326-5/fulltext

### Learning Bias

Learning bias arises when modeling choices amplify performance disparities across different examples in the data. For example, an important modeling choice is the main criterion (also known as objective function) that an ML algorithm learns to optimize during training. Typically, these functions prioritize accuracy. However, issues can arise when prioritizing one objective (e.g., overall accuracy) damages another (e.g., disparate impact)[10]. For example, minimizing error when building a model to determine probability of default might inadvertently lead to a model with more false positives than might be desirable in many contexts.

## Figure 37: Customer Income Distribution

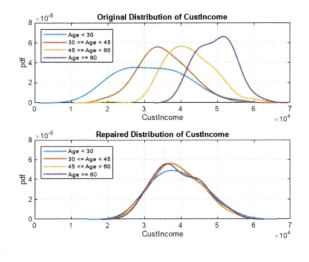

---

[10] https://www.mathworks.com/help/risk/bias-mitigation-for-credit-scoring-model-by-disparate-impact-removal.html

### Evaluation Bias

Evaluation bias occurs when the benchmark data used for a particular task **does not represent the population the model is actually used on**. A model is optimized on its training data, but its quality is often measured on benchmarks (e.g., UCI datasets, Faces in the Wild, ImageNet). This issue operates at a broader scale than other sources of bias: a misrepresentative benchmark encourages the development and deployment of models that perform well only on the subset of the data represented by the benchmark data.

For example, the Gender Shades paper[11] discovered that two widely used facial analysis benchmark datasets (IJB-A[12] and Adience[13]) were primarily composed of lighter-skinned subjects (79.6% and 86.2%, respectively). The authors of the paper evaluated 3 commercial gender classification systems using those datasets and showed that darker-skinned females were the most misclassified group (with error rates of up to 34.7%). The maximum error rate for lighter-skinned males is 0.8%. The substantial disparities in the accuracy of classifying darker females, lighter females, darker males, and lighter males) classification systems require urgent attention if commercial companies are to build genuinely fair, transparent and accountable facial analysis algorithms.

---

11

http://proceedings.mlr.press/v81/buolamwini18a/buolamwini18a.pdf
[12] https://paperswithcode.com/dataset/ijb-a
[13] https://paperswithcode.com/dataset/adience

## Figure 38: Facial Recognition Accuracy

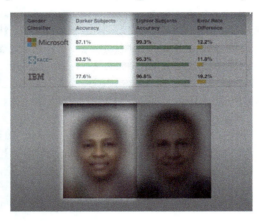

| Gender Classifier | Darker Subjects Accuracy | Lighter Subjects Accuracy | Error Rate Difference |
|---|---|---|---|
| Microsoft | 87.1% | 99.3% | 12.2% |
| FACE+ | 83.5% | 95.3% | 11.8% |
| IBM | 77.6% | 96.8% | 19.2% |

## Deployment Bias

Deployment bias arises when there is a mismatch between the problem a model is intended to solve and the way in which it is actually used. For example, the criminal justice system uses tools to predict the likelihood that a convicted criminal will relapse into criminal behavior. However, the predictions are not designed for judges when deciding appropriate punishments at the time of sentencing. If used in that way, it could cause unexpected harm.

**Key Takeaways**

Different Sources of Biases from AI models

- Historical: Historical data may be accurate but is biased
- Representations: Development Data does not represent adequately some part of population the model will be applied to
- Measurement: Bias in choosing, collecting, or computing features and labels
- Aggregation: One-size-fits-all is used for data when underlying groups or types of examples should be considered differently
- Learning: When modeling choices amplify performance disparities across different examples in the data
- Evaluation: When benchmark data used for a particular task does not represent the population the model is used on
- Deployment: Mismatch between the problem the model is intended to solve and way it is actually used

# Chapter 9: AI Principles

*"To live with change, to optimize change, you need principles that don't change." -- Stephen R. Covey*

As we discussed in the earlier chapters, AI has the potential to change our lives in remarkable ways: To improve the welfare and well-being of people, to contribute to positive sustainable global economic activity, to increase innovation and productivity, and to help respond to key global challenges. It is deployed in many sectors ranging from production, finance and transport to healthcare and security.

In true meaning of the saying "Something's gotta give," AI also presents challenges for our societies, in economies, inequalities, implications for democracy and human rights etc.

Taking these into consideration, the Organization for Economic Cooperation and Development (OECD) has undertaken empirical and policy activities on AI over the past two years, starting with a Technology Foresight Forum on AI in 2016 and an international conference on AI: Intelligent Machines, Smart Policies in 2017. The Organization also conducted analytical and measurement work that provides an overview of the AI technical landscape, maps economic and social impacts of AI technologies and their applications, identifies major policy considerations, and describes AI initiatives from governments and other stakeholders at national and international levels.

This work has demonstrated the need to shape a stable policy environment at the international level to foster trust in and adoption of AI in society. OECD developed a set of AI Principles taking these into consideration to promote use of AI that is innovative and trustworthy and that respects human rights and democratic values while being practical and flexible enough to stand the test of time.US is one of the 42 countries that adopted the OECD principles on AI at the government level.

Many organizations have also developed their own AI principles but they are mostly some variations of the principles described below:

## Figure 39: OECD Principles

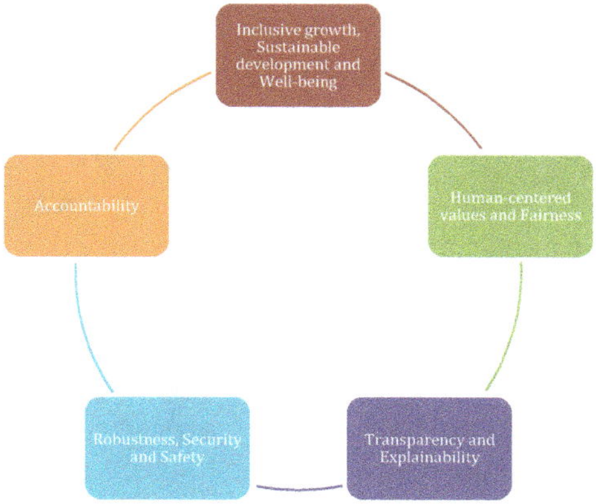

**(Principle 1.1)** Inclusive growth, sustainable development and well-**being**

*This Principle highlights the potential for trustworthy AI to contribute to overall growth and prosperity for all –*

*individuals, society, and planet – and advance global development objectives.*

Stakeholders should proactively engage in responsible stewardship of trustworthy AI in pursuit of beneficial outcomes for people and the planet, such as augmenting human capabilities and enhancing creativity, advancing inclusion of underrepresented populations, reducing economic, social, gender and other inequalities, and protecting natural environments, thus invigorating inclusive growth, sustainable development and well-being.

### (Principle 1.2) Human-centered values and fairness

*AI systems should be designed in a way that respects the rule of law, human rights, democratic values and diversity, and should include appropriate safeguards to ensure a fair and just society.*

AI actors should respect the rule of law, human rights and democratic values, throughout the AI system lifecycle. These include freedom, dignity and autonomy, privacy and data protection, non-discrimination and equality, diversity, fairness, social justice, and internationally recognized labor rights.

To this end, AI actors should implement mechanisms and safeguards, such as capacity for human determination, that are appropriate to the context and consistent with the state of art.

### (Principle 1.3) Transparency and explainability

*This principle is about transparency and responsible disclosure around AI systems to ensure that people understand when they are engaging with them and can challenge outcomes.*

AI Actors should commit to transparency and responsible disclosure regarding AI systems. To this end, they should provide meaningful information, appropriate to the context, and consistent with the state of art: to foster a general understanding of AI systems, to make stakeholders aware of their interactions with AI systems, including in the workplace, to enable those affected by an AI system to understand the outcome, and, to enable those adversely affected by an AI system to challenge its outcome based on plain and easy-to-understand information on the factors, and the logic that served as the basis for the prediction, recommendation or decision.

### (Principle 1.4) Robustness, security and safety

*AI systems must function in a robust, secure and safe way throughout their lifetimes, and potential risks should be continually assessed and managed*

AI systems should be robust, secure and safe throughout their entire lifecycle so that, in conditions of normal use, foreseeable use or misuse, or other adverse conditions, they function appropriately and do not pose unreasonable safety risk.

To this end, AI actors should ensure traceability, including in relation to datasets, processes and decisions made during the AI system lifecycle, to enable analysis of the AI system's outcomes and responses to inquiry, appropriate to the context and consistent with the state of art.

AI actors should, based on their roles, the context, and their ability to act, apply a systematic risk management approach to each phase of the AI system lifecycle on a continuous basis to address risks related to AI systems, including privacy, digital security, safety and bias.

### (Principle 1.5) Accountability

*Organizations and individuals developing, deploying or operating AI systems should be held accountable for their proper functioning in line with the OECD's values-based principles for AI.*

AI actors should be accountable for the proper functioning of AI systems and for the respect of the above principles, based on their roles, the context, and consistent with the state of art.

Below table shows the AI Principles adopted by some of the large tech companies. The table demonstrates that the principles have similar themes and are quite consistent with each other.

**Table 8: Comparison of AI Principles of Top AI Firms**

| Principle | OECD[14] | Google[15] | Microsoft[16] | IBM[17] | META[18] | Salesforce[19] |
|---|---|---|---|---|---|---|
| Inclusive Growth, Sustainable development | ✓ | ✓ | ✓ | | | ✓ |
| Human-centered values and fairness | ✓ | ✓ | ✓ | ✓ | ✓ | ✓ |

---

[14] https://oecd.ai/en/ai-principles

[15] https://ai.google/responsibility/principles/

[16] https://www.microsoft.com/en-us/ai/responsible-ai

[17] https://www.ibm.com/blog/a-framework-to-render-ai-principles-actionable/

[18] https://ai.meta.com/responsible-ai/

[19] https://blog.salesforceairesearch.com/meet-salesforces-trusted-ai-principles/

| | | | | | |
|---|---|---|---|---|---|
| **Transparency and Explainability** | ✓ | ✓ | ✓ | ✓ | ✓ | ✓ |
| **Robustness, Security and Safety** | ✓ | ✓ | ✓ | ✓ | ✓ | ✓ |
| **Accountability** | ✓ | ✓ | ✓ | ✓ | ✓ | ✓ |
| **Scientific Excellence** | | | ✓ | ✓ | ✓ | ✓ |
| **Privacy** | | ✓ | ✓ | ✓ | ✓ | |
| **Empowering** | | | | | | ✓ |

**Table 9: Verbiage of AI Principles of Top AI Firms**

| Google[15] | Microsoft[16] | IBM[17] | META[18] | Salesforce[19] |
|---|---|---|---|---|
| Be socially beneficial. | Fairness | Explainability | Privacy & Security | Responsible |
| Avoid creating or reinforcing unfair bias. | Reliability & Safety | Fairness | Fairness & Inclusion | Inclusive |
| Be accountable to people. | Privacy & Security | Robustness | Robustness & Safety | Accountable |
| Incorporate privacy design principles. | Inclusiveness | Transparency | Transparency & Control | Transparent |
| Uphold high standards of scientific excellence | Transparency | Privacy | Accountability & Governance | Empowering |
| | Accountability | | | |

By reviewing the different principles going from OECD to other large AI/ML companies, other companies that are developing their principles can customize their own principles by focusing on their value propositions.

In the next chapter I discuss how AI regulations are being proposed all over the world and how companies can use their principles and develop a risk management framework.

**Key Takeaways**

OECD AI Principles is foundation for most companies AI Principles

- Inclusive growth, sustainable development and well-Being
- Human-centered values and fairness
- Transparency and explainability
- Robustness, security and safety
- Accountability

# Chapter 10: AI Regulations and Governance

*"Three laws of robotics: The first law is that a robot shall not harm a human, or by inaction allow a human to come to harm. The second law is that a robot shall obey any instruction given to it by a human, and the third law is that a robot shall avoid actions or situations that could cause it to come to harm itself.." – Isaac Asimov*

Artificial intelligence (AI) is the new subject of large-scale regulation by governments around the world. While AI has many benefits, such as increased productivity and cost savings, it also presents some risks and challenges as we noted in earlier chapters. AI systems can sometimes be biased or discriminatory, leading to unfair outcomes or they can raise concerns about privacy and data security, as these systems often rely on large amounts of personal data.

As a result, governments around the world are starting to introduce regulations to ensure that AI is developed and used in a safe, responsible, and ethical manner. These regulations cover a range of issues, from data privacy and security to algorithmic transparency and accountability.

This chapter describes AI regulation in the U.S., EU, Canada, and China and how each country approaches the technology as they seek to balance economic, social, and public priorities with innovation.

### European Union: Artificial Intelligence Act (AIA)

The European Union introduced the Artificial Intelligence Act (AIA) on April 21, 2021 and approved by the parliament on June 14, 2023. The text proposes a risk-based approach to guide the use of AI in both the private and public sectors. The approach defines three risk categories: unacceptable risk applications, high-risk applications, and applications not explicitly banned. The regulation prohibits the use of AI in critical services that could threaten livelihoods or encourage destructive behavior. However, it allows the technology to be used in other sensitive sectors, such as health, with maximum safety and efficacy checks by regulators. The legislation is still under review in the European Parliament.

The AI Act is a type of legislation that regulates all automated technology rather than specific areas of concern. It defines AI systems to include a wide range of automated decision-makers, such as algorithms, machine learning tools, and logic tools, even though some of these technologies are not considered AI.

### Canada: The Artificial Intelligence and Data Act (AIDA)

In June of 2022, Canadian Parliament introduced a draft regulatory framework for Artificial Intelligence using a modified risk-based approach.

The bill has three pillars, but this piece will just examine the section dealing with AI, the Artificial Intelligence and Data Act (AIDA). The goal of AIDA is to standardize private companies' design and development of AI across the provinces and territories.

The modified risk-based approach is different from the EU's approach as it does not ban the use of automated decision-making tools, even in critical areas. Instead, under the AIDA regulation, developers must create a mitigation plan to reduce risks and increase transparency when using AI in high-risk systems. The plan should ensure that the tools do not violate anti-discrimination laws. These mitigation plans or impact assessments aim to decrease risk and increase transparency in the use of AI in social, business, and political systems.

### United States: AI Bill of Rights and State Initiatives

The United States has yet to pass federal legislation governing AI applications. Instead, the Biden Administration and the National Institute of Standards and Technology (NIST) have published broad AI guidance for the safe use of AI. In addition, state and city governments are pursuing their own regulations and task forces for AI use. In a break from the EU model, regulation thus far targets specific use cases rather than seeking to regulate AI technology as a whole.

At the federal level, the Biden Administration recently released the AI Bill of Rights, which addresses concerns about AI misuse and provides recommendations for safely using AI tools in both the public and private sectors. This AI strategy would not be legally binding. Instead, the Bill of Rights calls for key safety strategies such as greater data privacy, protections against algorithmic discrimination, and guidance on how to prioritize safe and effective AI tools. While the blueprint is not legally binding, it serves as a guide for lawmakers at all levels of government who are considering AI regulation.

In addition, NIST, which is an agency in the Department of Commerce that develops technology standards, published standards for managing AI bias. NIST also tracks how the public sector integrates AI tools across the federal government.

In 2022, 15 states and localities proposed or passed legislation concerning AI. Some bills focus on regulating AI tools in the private sector, while others set standards for public-sector AI use. New York City introduced one of the first AI laws in the U.S., effective from January 2023, which aims to prevent AI bias in the employment process. Colorado and Vermont created task forces to study AI applications, such as facial recognition, at the state level.

In April 2023, California lawmakers proposed a bill on the oversight of artificial intelligence that would monitor how employers and industries use automated decision tools, from algorithms that filter out job applicants to programs that detect academic cheating.

### China: Algorithm Transparency and Promoting AI Industry Development

China has set a goal for the private AI industry to make $154 billion annually by 2030. China has yet to pass rules on AI technology at large. Recently, however, the country introduced a law that regulates how private companies use online algorithms for consumer marketing. The law requires companies to inform users of AI for marketing purposes and bans the use of customer financial data to advertise the same product at different prices. However, not surprisingly, the law does not apply to the Chinese government's use of AI.

Along with China's federal regulation, in September of 2022, Shanghai became the first province to pass a law focused on private-sector AI development. The law titled Shanghai Regulations on Promoting the Development of the AI Industry provides a framework for companies in the region to develop their AI products in line with non-Chinese AI regulations.

### Next Steps for Global Regulation:

Artificial intelligence is a promising tool that is stimulating global growth and driving the future of innovation. Despite the positive impacts of AI, it is not a surprise that even the godfather of AI, Jeffrey Hinton[20] and creators of some of AI applications are calling for some regulation to combat the misuse of AI and to protect consumers.

The different approaches summed in this chapter offer methodologies for how policymakers around

---

[20] Geoffrey Hinton was an artificial intelligence pioneer. In 2012, Dr. Hinton and two of his graduate students at the University of Toronto created technology that became the intellectual foundation for the A.I. systems that the tech industry's biggest companies believe is a key to their future.

the world are approaching specific harms from AI, as well as AI as a whole. The EU's approach regulates the use of any automated decision-making tools and outlines the sectors where they can and cannot be used. The U.S. offers voluntary recommendations and standards at the federal level, with states and cities pursuing their own targeted studies and rules based on specific harms. The modified risk-based approach in Canada regulates all AI tools but stops short of banning the technology in certain spheres by allowing companies to define their own risk-mitigation strategies. And the Chinese approach seeks to increase transparency for consumers and become a global power in AI standards.

To prepare, companies will need to further develop global stances on AI ethics and compliance for their products in order to meet transforming regulations. In addition, legislators should focus on legitimate harms to consumers and keep apprised of how stricter regulatory regimes affect AI innovation which brings us to the next section.

### NIST AI Risk Management Framework

On January 26, 2023, the National Institute of Standards and Technology (NIST) published new guidance,[21] the AI Risk Management Framework (AI RMF) that seeks to cultivate trust in AI technologies and promote AI innovation while mitigating risk. The framework is a guidance document for voluntary use by organizations designing, developing, deploying or using AI

---

[21] https://www.nist.gov/news-events/news/2023/01/nist-risk-management-framework-aims-improve-trustworthiness-artificial

systems to help manage the many risks of AI technologies.

The AI RMF follows a direction from Congress for NIST to develop the framework and was produced in close collaboration with the private and public sectors. It is intended to adapt to the AI landscape as technologies continue to develop, and to be used by organizations in varying degrees and capacities so that society can benefit from AI technologies while also being protected from its potential harms.

The framework offers four interrelated functions as a risk mitigation method: govern, map, measure, and manage.

**Figure 40: NIST Risk Management Framework**

**"Govern"** sits at the core of the RMF's mitigation strategy, and is intended to serve as a foundational culture of risk prevention and management bedrocking for any organization using the RMF.

Building atop the "Govern" foundation, **"Map"** comes next in the RMF game-plan. This step works to contextualize potential risks in an AI technology, and broadly identify the positive mission and uses of any given AI system, while simultaneously taking into account its limitations.

This context should then allow framework users to **"Measure"** how an AI system actually functions. Crucial to the "Measure" component is employing sufficient metrics that represent universal scientific and ethical norms. Strong measuring is then applied through "rigorous" software testing, further analyzed by external experts and user feedback.

"Potential pitfalls when seeking to measure negative risk or harms include the reality that development of metrics is often an institutional endeavor and may inadvertently reflect factors unrelated to the underlying impact," the NIST AI Risk Management report cautions. "Measuring AI risks includes tracking metrics for trustworthy characteristics, social impact and human-AI configurations."

The final step in the AI RMF mitigation strategy is **"Manage,"** whose main function is to allocate risk mitigation resources and ensure that previously established mechanisms are continuously implemented.

"Framework users will enhance their capacity to comprehensively evaluate system trustworthiness, identify and track existing and emergent risks and verify efficacy of the metrics," the report states.

The Framework articulates the following characteristics of trustworthy AI and offers guidance for addressing them. Characteristics of trustworthy AI systems are closely aligned with the AI Principles discussed in the previous chapter and include:

- valid and reliable
- safe, secure and resilient
- accountable and transparent
- explainable and interpretable
- privacy-enhanced
- fair with harmful bias managed

Creating trustworthy AI requires balancing each of these characteristics based on the AI system's context of use. While all characteristics are socio-technical system attributes, accountability and transparency also relate to the processes and activities internal to an AI system and its external setting. Neglecting these characteristics can increase the probability and magnitude of negative consequences.

The AI Risk Management Framework proposed by NIST also has a playbook that can be used to operationalize the risk management framework. You can find the playbook in the link below:

https://airc.nist.gov/AI_RMF_Knowledge_Base/Playbook

## Key Takeaways

Most notable AI regulations under development are

- European Union Artificial Intelligence Act
- Canada's Artificial Intelligence and Data Act
- United States's AI Bill of Rights and State Initiatives
- China's Algorithm Transparency and Promoting AI Industry Development

National Institute of Standards and Technology (NIST) has published the risk management framework for artificial intelligence (AI RMF) which has four functions as a risk management method:

- Govern - intended to serve as a foundational culture of risk prevention and management bedrocking for any organization using the RMF
- Map - works to contextualize potential risks in an AI technology, and broadly identify the positive mission and uses of any given AI system, while simultaneously taking into account its limitations
- Measure - employs metrics that represent universal scientific and ethical norms
- Manage - main function is to allocate risk mitigation resources and ensure that previously established mechanisms are continuously implemented

# Chapter 11: ChatGPT, Bard and Other Generative AI Tools

*"Any sufficiently advanced technology is indistinguishable from magic."— Arthur C Clarke*

### ChatGPT

You must have heard or perhaps experimented with ChatGPT that was launched in November 2022. ChatGPT is a natural language processing tool driven by AI technology that allows you to have human-like conversations and much more like writing code in any language with a chatbot. It is from the family of Generative AI models. Generative AI enables users to generate new content based on a variety of inputs. The inputs and outputs to these models can include text, images, sounds, or other types of data.

I asked ChatGPT to write me a limerick on the Amazon Rainforest. See the response below

## Figure 41: ChatGPT Example 1: Limerick

I then asked it to write me Python code for binary search. See the response below

## Figure 42: ChatGPT Example 2: Generate Code

Powerful! Isn't it?

ChatGPT comes from the family of language models. The name "ChatGPT" combines "Chat", referring to its chatbot functionality, and "GPT", which stands for Generative Pre-trained22 Transformer, a type of large language model (LLM). LLMs are deep learning algorithms that can recognize, summarize, translate, predict, and generate content using very large datasets.

Google and Wolfram Alpha also interact with users via a single line text entry field and provide text results. Google returns search results, a list of web pages and articles that will provide information related to the search queries. Wolfram Alpha generally provides mathematical and data analysis-related answers.

ChatGPT, by contrast, provides a response based on the context and intent behind a user's question. You can't, for example, ask Google to write a story or ask Wolfram Alpha to write a code module, but ChatGPT can perform these tasks, and in many instances, in a convincing and impressive manner.

So how is ChatGPT different from Google or Wolfram Alpha? Well, Google search's power is the ability to do enormous database lookups and

---

[22] Pre-trained means the model was previously trained on some data like we saw in the earlier chapters

provide a series of matches. Wolfram Alpha's power is the ability to parse data-related questions and perform calculations based on those questions. ChatGPT's power, on the other hand, is the ability to parse queries and produce fully fleshed out answers and results based on most of the world's digitally-accessible text-based information -- at least information that existed as of its time of training (e.g., prior to 2021 for ChatGPT 3).

In this chapter, we will examine how ChatGPT can produce those fully fleshed out answers. We will start by looking at the main phases of ChatGPT operation, then cover some of the core AI architecture components that make it all work.

The two main phases of Google search are spidering and data gathering. Similarly, the two main phases of ChatGPT operation are pre-training (which is the data gathering) and transformer learning (which provides answers in a human dialog format).

Pre-training the AI

As we saw in previous chapters, AIs use two principal approaches: supervised and unsupervised. The supervised approach was used for most AI projects related to language processing, up until the current examples of generative AI systems like ChatGPT.

Supervised pre-training is a process where a model is trained on a labeled dataset, where each input is associated with a corresponding output, as we saw earlier.

For example, an AI could be trained on a dataset of customer service conversations, where the user's questions and complaints are labeled with the appropriate responses from the customer service representative. To train the AI, questions like "How can I reset my password?" would be provided as user input, and answers like "You can reset your password by visiting the account settings page on our website and following the prompts" would be provided as output.

In a supervised training approach, the overall model is trained to learn a mapping function that can map inputs to outputs accurately. This process is used in supervised learning tasks, such as classification and regression as we saw in the earlier chapters.

As you might imagine, there are limits to how this can scale since human trainers tasked with labeling would have to anticipate multitudes of scenarios for all the inputs and outputs. Training could take a very long time and be limited in subject matter expertise.

But as we've come to know, ChatGPT has very few limits in subject matter expertise. This is where unsupervised pre-training comes into play.

Unsupervised pre-training as we saw earlier, is the process by which a model is trained on data where no specific output is associated with each input. Instead, the model is trained to learn the underlying structure and patterns in the input data without any specific task in mind. In the context of language modeling, non-supervised pre-training can be used to train a model to understand the syntax and semantics of natural language, so that it can generate coherent and meaningful text in a conversational context.

It's here where ChatGPT's apparently limitless knowledge becomes possible. Because the developers don't need to know the outputs that come from the inputs, all they have to do is dump more and more information into the ChatGPT pre-training mechanism, which is called transformer-base language modeling.

Transformer architecture

The transformer architecture is a type of neural network that is used for processing natural language data. A neural network as we saw earlier, simulates the way a human brain works by processing information through layers of interconnected nodes.

The transformer architecture processes sequences of words to understand the context and the relationships between the words (refer to Chapter 3 on Natural Language Processing).

During training, the transformer is given input data, such as a sentence, and is asked to make a prediction based on that input. The model is updated based on how well its prediction matches the actual output. Through this process, the transformer learns to understand the context and relationships between words in a sequence, making it a powerful tool for natural language processing tasks such as language translation and text generation.

Below is the description of the data that gets fed into ChatGPT.

ChatGPT's training datasets

ChatGPT was trained on a huge dataset called WebText2, a library of over 45 terabytes of text data with approximately 175 billion parameters23! This massive amount of data allowed ChatGPT to learn patterns and relationships between words and

---

[23] Parameters are the weights in the layers in a neural network as discussed in Chapter 6

phrases in natural language at an unprecedented scale, which is one of the reasons why it is so effective at generating coherent and contextually relevant responses to user queries.

While ChatGPT is based on the GPT-3 architecture, it has been fine-tuned on a different dataset and optimized for conversational use cases. This allows it to provide a more personalized and engaging experience for users who interact with it through a chat interface.

For example, OpenAI (developers of ChatGPT) has released a dataset called Persona-Chat that is specifically designed for training conversational AI models like ChatGPT. This dataset consists of over 160,000 dialogues between two human participants, with each participant assigned a unique persona that describes their background, interests, and personality. This allows ChatGPT to learn how to generate responses that are personalized and relevant to the specific context of the conversation.

In addition to Persona-Chat, there are many other conversational datasets that were used to fine-tune ChatGPT. Here are a few examples:

Cornell Movie Dialogs Corpus: a dataset containing conversations between characters in movie scripts. It includes over 200,000 conversational exchanges between more than 10,000 movie character pairs, covering a diverse range of topics and genres.

Ubuntu Dialogue Corpus: a collection of multi-turn dialogues between users seeking technical support and the Ubuntu community support team. It contains over 1 million dialogues, making it one of the largest publicly available datasets for research on dialog systems.

DailyDialog: a collection of human-to-human dialogues in a variety of topics, ranging from daily life conversations to discussions about social issues. Each dialogue in the dataset consists of several turns, and is labeled with a set of emotion, sentiment, and topic information.

In addition to these datasets, ChatGPT was trained on a large amount of unstructured data found on the internet, including websites, books, and other text sources. This allowed ChatGPT to learn about the structure and patterns of language in a more general sense, which could then be fine-tuned for specific applications like dialogue management or sentiment analysis.

ChatGPT is a distinct model that was trained using a similar approach as the GPT series, but with some differences in architecture and training data. ChatGPT version 4 has 1.5 trillion parameters, which is even larger than GPT-3's 175 billion parameters.

Overall, the training data used to fine-tune ChatGPT is typically conversational in nature and specifically curated to include dialogues between humans, which allows ChatGPT to learn how to generate natural and engaging responses in a conversational format.

So essentially ChatGPT was fed a lot of data and left to its own devices to find patterns and make sense of it all. This is the mechanism that allowed the new generative AI systems to scale up so quickly.

While the heavy lifting for ChatGPT's generative AI is being done by the pre-training, it also has to be able to understand questions and construct answers from all that data. That's done by the inference phase which consists of natural language processing and dialog management.

Google Bard

Google's Bard is based on the LaMDA (Language Model for Dialogue Application) language model, trained on datasets based on Internet content called Infiniset. Infiniset is a blend of Internet content that was deliberately chosen to enhance the model's ability to engage in dialogue.

The 2022 LaMDA research paper lists percentages of different kinds of data used to train LaMDA, but only 12.5% comes from a public dataset of crawled content from the web and another 12.5% comes from Wikipedia.

In total, LaMDA was pre-trained on 137 billion parameters and with 1.56 trillion words of "public dialog data and web text."

The dataset is comprised of the following mix:

- 12.5% C424-based data

- 12.5% English language Wikipedia

- 12.5% code documents from programming Q&A websites, tutorials, and others

- 6.25% English web documents

- 6.25% Non-English web documents

- 50% dialogs data from public forums

The first two parts of Infiniset (C4 and Wikipedia) is comprised of data that is known.

---

[24] C4 is a colossal, cleaned version of Common Crawl's web crawl corpus. It was based on Common Crawl dataset: https://commoncrawl.org.

The C4 dataset, which will be explored shortly, is a specially filtered version of the Common Crawl dataset.

Only 25% of the data is from a named source (the C4 dataset and Wikipedia). The rest of the data that makes up the bulk of the Infiniset dataset, 75%, consists of words that were scraped from the Internet.

The research paper doesn't say how the data was obtained from websites, what websites it was obtained from or any other details about the scraped content.

Google only uses generalized descriptions like "Non-English web documents."

C4 is a dataset developed by Google in 2020. C4 stands for "Colossal Clean Crawled Corpus." This dataset is based on the Common Crawl data, which is an open-source dataset.

Common Crawl is a registered non-profit organization that crawls the Internet on a monthly basis to create free datasets that anyone can use. The Common Crawl organization is currently run by people who have worked for the Wikimedia Foundation, former Googlers, a founder of Blekko, and count as advisors people like Peter Norvig, Director of Research at Google and Danny Sullivan (also of Google).

The raw Common Crawl data is cleaned up by removing things like thin content, obscene words, lorem ipsum, navigational menus, deduplication, etc. in order to limit the dataset to the main content.

The point of filtering out unnecessary data was to remove gibberish and retain examples of natural English.

Fifty percent of the training data comes from "dialogs data from public forums,"which may include Reddit, StackOverflow etc.

Reddit is used in many important datasets such as ones developed by OpenAI called WebText2 (PDF), an open-source approximation of WebText2 called OpenWebText2 and Google's own WebText-like (PDF) dataset from 2020.

Google also published details of another dataset of public dialog sites a month before the publication of the LaMDA paper.

There are other Generative AI tools besides ChatGPT and Bard and the table below25 compares the most common ones at the moment

25 Source: https://www.eweek.com/artificial-intelligence/generative-ai-apps-tools/#comparison_chart

**Table 10: Comparison of Large Language Models**

| Tool | Company | Use Case(s) | Starting Price |
|------|---------|-------------|----------------|
| **GPT-4** | OpenAI | Large Language Model (LLM) | |
| **ChatGPT** | OpenAI | Chatbot, Content Generation | **Consumer access:** Currently free **Model access:** $0.002 per 1,000 tokens |
| **AlphaCode** | DeepMind (Alphabet) | LLM-Powered Coding | Free |
| **GitHub Copilot** | Microsoft/GitHub/OpenAI | Code Generation | $10 per month, or $100 per year |

| | | | |
|---|---|---|---|
| **Bard** | Google (Alphabet) | Chatbot, Content Generation | Currently free and available to a small group of users |
| **Cohere Generate** | Cohere | Large Language Model (LLM), content Generation | Free |
| **Claude** | Anthropic | Large Language Model (LLM), Content Generation, AI Assistant | **Prompt:** $1.63 per million tokens<br><br>**Completion:** $5.51 per million tokens |
| **Synthesia** | Synthesia | Video Creation | $30 per month, billed monthly |

| DALL-E 2 | OpenAI | Image and Art Generation | 115 credits for $15 USD |
|----------|--------|--------------------------|-------------------------|

## Key Takeaways

- Generative AI is from a family of AI models that enables users to generate new content based on a variety of inputs. The inputs and outputs to these models can include text, images, sounds, or other types of data.
- Most common Generative AI tools are Open AI's ChatGPT and Google's Bard.
- ChatGPT stands for Generative Pretrained Transformer which is a type of Large Language Models
- Training sets used for generative AI models include publicly available text datasets such as from internet websites, books and other text sources.

# *Glossary*

| | |
|---|---|
| AI | The simulation of human intelligence in machines that are programmed to think like humans and mimic their actions. |
| ANN | Artificial Neural Networks mimic the human brain through a set of algorithms |
| Benchmark | evaluate or check (something) by comparison with a standard |
| ChatGPT | Chat Generative Pre-trained Transformer model by OpenAI that allows human like interactions with a chatbot |
| CNN | Convolutional Neural Network is analogous to that of the connectivity pattern of Neurons in the Human Brain and was inspired by the organization of the Visual Cortex |
| FFNN | Feed Forward Neural Network is a network where data flows from the input layer to the output layer without going backward |
| Google Bard | Large language model by Google that allows you to have human like interactions through a chatbot |
| Input layer | The very beginning of the workflow for the artificial neural network |

| | |
|---|---|
| Large Language Model (LLM) | Deep learning algorithms that can recognize, summarize, translate, predict, and generate content using very large datasets |
| Logistic regression | a statistical method for analyzing a dataset in which there are one or more independent variables that determine an outcome. The outcome is measured with a dichotomous variable (in which there are only two possible outcomes) |
| ML | Machine Learning is a derivative of sorts of AI where you use historical data as input into an algorithm to *predict* new output values |
| Neural network | Can refer to either ANN or network of neurons in a living creature |
| NIST | National Institute of Standards and Technology. NIST recently published their AI Risk Management Framework |
| NLP | Natural Language Processing is a machine learning technology that gives computers the ability to interpret, manipulate, and comprehend human language |
| Output Layer | The final layer in the neural network where desired predictions are obtained |

| | |
|---|---|
| quant | an expert at analyzing and managing quantitative data |
| Reinforcement Learning | In reinforcement learning, developers devise a method of rewarding desired behaviors and punishing negative behaviors |
| RNN | Recurrent Neural Network |
| ROC | Receiver Operating Characteristic used in gauging the effectiveness of classification problems. |
| Supervised Learning | In supervised learning, the algorithm learns from the training dataset. Since the correct answers are known the algorithm iteratively makes predictions on the training data |

# Note from the Author

Thank you for reading this book. If you enjoyed reading it, please consider leaving a review on Amazon.com.

I would love to hear from you. You can find me on LinkedIn.


Best,
Aruna Joshi

# About the Author

Aruna Joshi has over two decades of experience in the financial services industry ranging from software engineering, insurance and banking. She has a Ph.D. In Mechanical Engineering and an MFE from UC Berkeley.

She is a frequent speaker at Model Risk related conferences and has published papers in reputable journals.

She lives in Menlo Park with her husband and has two adult daughters.

# Acknowledgements

Many individuals played a significant role in making this book possible. First and foremost, I would like to thank my husband, Arun Majumdar whose persistence converted a dream of this book into reality.

He along with my sister, Sunanda Chatterjee, and my friend Ajit Mayya– none of whom are active in the field of AI and ML— provided valuable feedback to make this book readable and understandable to individuals who are new to this exciting area.

I would also like to thank Stefaan D'Hoore, my manager who always challenges me to dig deeper when validating the models. Finally, I'd like to thank my parents, Avinash and Mandakini Joshi, for their constant encouragement

# Other books by Aruna Joshi

**Managing Risk of Financial Models: A smart and
simple guide for the practitioner**

This book is a simple, step-by-step guide to how
top institutions determine what is a model, how to
identify, assess, and mitigate model risk, and how
to report to senior management.

Using practical examples, this book gives an
overview of the state of the art methods applied in
establishing and maintaining a strong model risk
management program at a financial institution.